Amulets of the Goddess

Mississauga Library System

Courtneypark

Amulets of the Goddess

Oracle of Ancient Wisdom

Nancy Blair

Wingbow Press
Oakland, California

Copyright © 1993 by Nancy Blair
All rights reserved.
Amulets of the Goddess™ is a trademark of Nancy Blair.

Manufactured in the United States of America.

Wingbow Press books are published and distributed by Bookpeople, 7900 Edgewater Drive, Oakland, California 94621.
Cover, package and interior design by Brenn Lea Pearson.
Interior illustrations by Leo Morrissey (LM) and Angela Biesecker (AB).
Sculpture reproductions and photos on the front cover and pages 4, 11, 43 and 44 courtesy of Star River Productions.
Photo rendering by Lysandwr McNary and Kelly Bonsall.
Printing and packaging by Interprint.

Grateful acknowledgement is made to the following for permsission to reprint previously published material.
An excerpt from *Circle of Stones* by Judith Duerk, © 1989 LuraMedia, Inc,. San Diego, California. Used by permission. Excerpt from *Pornography and Silence* by Susan Griffin. Copyright © 1981 by Susan Griffin. Reprinted by permission of HarperCollins Publishers. "Rainbow Revelation" by Yoko Ono. Copyright © 1985 Ono Music. All rights administered by Sony Music Publishing, 8 Music Square West, Nashville, TN 37203. All rights reserved. Used by permission. *Healing Wise: The Second Wise Woman Herbal* by Susun Weed. Copyright © 1989 by Susun Weed. Reprinted by permission of Ash Tree Publishing. From *Maria Sabina and Her Mazatec Mushroom Velada* by R. Gordon Wasson, George Cowan, Florence Cowan and Willard Rhodes. Copyright © 1974 by R. Gordon Wasson, reprinted by permission of Harcourt Brace Jovanovich.

Library of Congress Catalog Card Number 92-35945
ISBN 0-914728-80-6

First edition August 1993

Some of the Amulets shown in this book are available for sale in pendant form; for more information, contact Star River Productions (see page 191 for address).

*For my mother
And for Earth, our source*

*May the Goddess heal our lives,
heal our world*

The Dreaming Goddess (page 63)	*The Gorgon Goddess* (page 67)	*Inanna* (page 73)	*The Laussel Goddess* (page 77)	*The Nile River Goddess* (page 82)
The Primal Mother and Child (page 86)	*The Dancing Bird Goddess* (page 90)	*Sheela-Na-Gig* (page 95)	*The Willendorf Goddess* (page 100)	*The Cat* (page 105)
The Cow (page 111)	*The Dolphin* (page 115)	*The Ewe* (page 118)	*The Frog* (page 122)	*The Owl* (page 125)
The Snake (page 130)	*The Sow* (page 136)	*The Spider* (page 141)	*The Comb* (page 147)	*Eyes* (page 152)
Hand With Seeds (page 155)	*The Labrys* (page 158)	*The Nightstar* (page 162)	*The Sprouting Seed* (page 165)	*The Temple* (page 168)
	The Triple Spiral (page 172)		*The Whirlwinds* (page 175)	

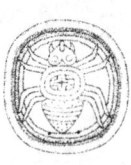

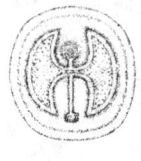

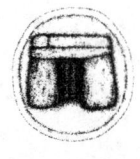

Contents

Acknowledgements .... *Page xi*
Introduction .... *Page 1*
Using Your Goddess Amulets .... *Page 15*
The Goddesses .... *Page 63*
   The Dreaming Goddess — Intuitive Inspiration .... Page 63
   Gorgon — Transforming Anger, Reclaiming Power .... Page 67
   Inanna, Awesome Queen — Self-Transformation .... Page 73
   The Laussel Goddess — Moon Time .... Page 77
   The Nile River Goddess — Strength, Triumph, Success .... Page 82
   The Primal Mother Goddess and Child — Infinite Love .... Page 86
   The Dancing Bird Goddess — Ecstasy .... Page 90
   Sheela-Na-Gig — Honoring Choices .... Page 95
   The Willendorf Goddess — Belonging .... Page 100
The Sacred Animals .... *Page 105*
   Cat — Protecting Good Fortune .... Page 105
   Cow — Uniting in Partnership .... Page 111
   Dolphin — Joy, Celebration .... Page 115
   Ewe — Self-Worth .... Page 118
   Frog — Speaking Out .... Page 122
   Owl — Wisdom of the Darkness .... Page 125
   Snake — Shedding Fear, Renewing Hope .... Page 130
   Sow — Listening .... Page 136
   Spider — Sacred Creativity .... Page 141

The Sacred Symbols .... *Page 147*
   Comb — Self-Reliance .... *Page 147*
   Eyes — Reflecting Inner Visions .... *Page 152*
   Hand With Seeds — Accepting Responsibility .... *Page 155*
   Labyris — Priestess Power .... *Page 158*
   Nightstar — Fulfillment .... *Page 162*
   Sprouting Seed — New Beginnings .... *Page 165*
   Temple — Breakthrough, Awakening, Healing .... *Page 168*
   Triple Spiral — Barriers, Boundaries and Possibilities ... *Page 172*
   Whirlwinds — Trusting the Invisible .... *Page 175*
Notes .... *Page 179*
Bibliography & Other Sources .... *Page 183*

Acknowledgements

I feel blessed to be able to express my gratitude to the many people who helped midwife this project into being.

My thanks first of all to my mother, Frances Blair, whose love, laughter and encouragement these past forty years have helped me understand the deep emotional power and strength of the mother/daughter bond. Thank you for allowing me the freedom to find my own way in the world. And special thanks for teaching me Yankee fortitude and your "down-to-earth," wise country ways, even when you thought I wasn't paying attention. And to the spirit of my father, Leo Blair, whose creative passion inspired my own. As an artist himself, he taught me how to see, not only with my eyes but with my soul.

I am deeply indebted to the many women and men whose research and insight into the Great Goddess came before me and which continue to guide my life in all ways. My deepest gratitude to Marija Gimbutas, Barbara Walker, Merlin Stone, Elinor Gadon, Starhawk, Riane Eisler, Vicki Noble, Hallie Iglehart Austen, Buffie Johnson, Alexander Marshack, James Mellaart, Susun Weed, Zsuzsanna Budapest, Susan Griffin, Shekhinah Mountainwater, Monica Sjöö, Barbara Mor, Layne Raymond, Susan Gale, and Diane Stein. Thanks still to so many others too numerous to mention.

Heartfelt thanks to Leo Morrissey, artist and friend, who like Inanna's faithful companion stood at the gate while I descended into the depths of the Underworld to retrieve and write "just one more sentence, one more page, one more chapter." Thank you for knowing when to come get me and when to start dinner without me. I also appreciated your careful attention to the details of illustration, drawing the Goddess images with the sensitivity and respect they deserve. Thank you for your undying patience while I made difficult editorial decisions about which images to include. Our love is a gift of the Goddess.

All healing is about remembering. Thanks to Michele Kelly, my Gemini friend and confidante who reminded me that "the Great Mama didn't bring you this far to drop you off" when the mental and emotional strain of writing a book *and* taking care of my business made me want to run away. Her healing words sustained my energy during the most difficult times.

Thanks to Joan Fericy for sharing her joy, enthusiasm and excitement for my creative ideas, aspirations and goals every Monday morning for the past year and a half. Our covenant of mutual support continues to strengthen my commitment to creativity, healing and personal growth. Thanks for reminding me to "give up the struggle."

I deeply appreciate the work of family and friends who helped me with the all too important details of pulling a project of this scope together. To my brother, Paul Blair, who unremittingly helped me get to know my new computer and the inevitable problems therein, with wit, humor and kindness. To my brother Leo Blair for his emotional support and heartfelt interest in my work. And thanks to John and Christine Blair for providing a "home base." To Angela Biesecker for her contributions to the illustrations. To Gale Sasson for remaining "on call," providing just the right feedback whenever I needed it. To Kathleen Willoughby for giving my first draft a careful reading. I appreciate so much her wise laughter and intelligent eye. To Pamela Novick for inspiring me with her music, poetry and dynamic Scorpionic energy.

Special thanks to Randy Fingland, my editor at Wingbow Press for his insightful and thought-provoking approach to this project. Most of my creative endeavors are done while in right brain "trance," and I am grateful for his many editorial suggestions along the way which helped me organize and ground my ideas. In particular, I appreciated his encouragement to include my personal experiences throughout the book. Thanks to all the people at Wingbow, especially Stanton Nelson, for taking great care in bringing my vision to life.

The stories I've included throughout the book are based on my personal experiences and those of friends and family. I've changed the details so that a story cannot be identified as belonging to one person. The integrity and essence remain true. Thanks to all the people who shared their personal healing stories in the many rituals and circles I attended over the years. Many blessings to all of you as you find your way back to the garden of the Goddess.

I am forever grateful that I followed my heart and pursued my path as an artist, learning how to trust my own creative process along the way. As complex, convoluted, unpredictable and ecstatic as it is, I have come to realize that sacred creativity is the magical life force of the Goddess flowing through me. And it is a gift I offer with love.

The transformative nature of the Goddess works in mysterious ways, always sustained by hope. I am an incurable optimist, and for this I am eternally grateful as I cast my vision into the future during these rapidly changing times and find myself standing eye to eye with Lilith, Goddess of radical transformation.

Let us imagine and co-create a better future together, and always...

May the Goddess be your guide,

Nancy Blair
June 6, 1992

Introduction

*In the beginning the Goddess was our Guide
Hers was the voice from Darkness
The unknown echoed within Her Earth Womb
Ancient dancers heard Her call
And Her rhythms counted time with the Moon*

In prehistoric cultures the world over, our ancestors carved and modeled amulets, charms and talismans from bone, stone, clay, wood and metal. Amulets were worn as personal adornments, used in celebration, divination and ritual, carried, rubbed and held tightly. They were decorated with symbols as a means of remaining in touch with life's often mysterious powers.

The earliest spiritual practices revolved around a direct attunement with a female life force, personified as a Great Goddess, Whose realm included the plants, animals, sea, sky and Earth—the entire cosmos. She was the first deity, Creatrix of all life, Source of perpetual renewal. She spoke through the Earth's seasons and the cycles of the female body. All life was imbued with Her divine and dynamic energy.

The images etched and modeled on the art and artifacts of these early cultures reflect a potent and spirited "language of the Goddess." In symbol and metaphor She empowered life, birth, death and regeneration. Celebrations, art, healing, dancing and sacred festivities were all in Her honor. Her presence guided the everyday lives of our early ancestors for tens of thousands of years prior to patriarchal religious and political domination.

It's important to note that Goddess Spirituality in prehistoric art and artifact did not reduce and fragment the nature of a

Handheld amulets from prehistoric Goddess cultures, worn as ornaments in ritual and teaching ceremonies or as timekeeping tools. All honored the sacred presence of a divine female Source. Drawings by Leo Morrissey.

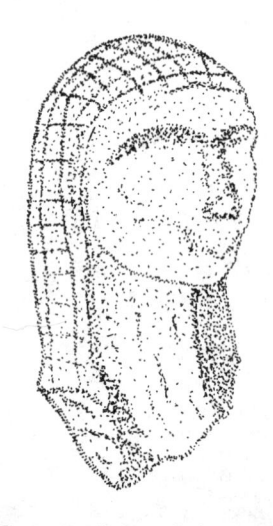

Goddess Head carved from mammoth ivory connects us to our Wise Woman heritage. Approximately 24,000 years old. France.

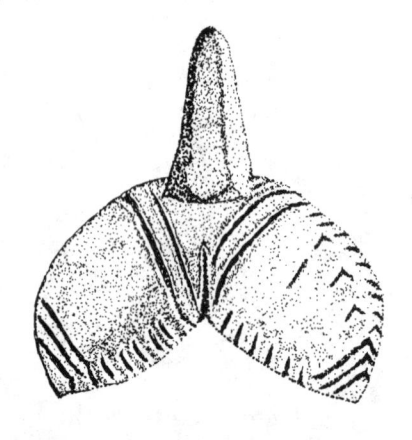

Breast amulet/pendant with chiseled markings on surface. This piece was found with six other breast pendant carvings and was probably worn as a necklace. Approximately 22,000 years old. Czechoslovakia.

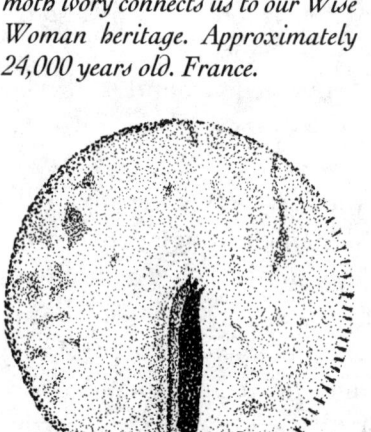

Vulva disk. Menstrual or birthing amulet with lunar notations on edge and rubbed with red ochre. Carved from mammoth tooth. Approximately 22,000 years old. Czechoslovakia.

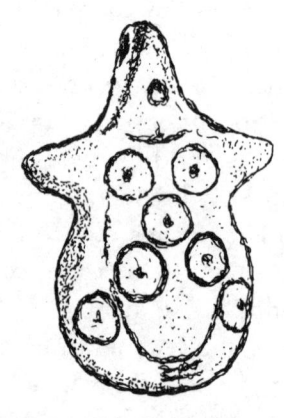

Goddess pendant with seven stamped dot and circle patterns. Do these indicate the body's seven "power centers"? Approximately 5,000 years old. Anatolia.

Amulets of the Goddess

Divine Creatrix to "body parts." Early peoples perceived the cosmic forces, as well as all life, as a unity. Goddess symbols, whether eyes, vulvas, breasts, footprints, handprints, meanders, spirals, energy symbols or snakes, embraced a "total picture." Today's Way of the Goddess is a healing process, first honoring the fragments, then putting them back together.

Awakening

When I entered graduate art school in my early thirties as an "older student," I was tired of critical jargon and an art history replete with male-identified symbols, perceptions and expressions that excluded or trivialized female art and expression. The art-school model of a "true artist" is a male genius who creates in isolation, suffers excruciating mental and emotional turmoil, eases his pain through self-destructive addictions and passions, dies in poverty, and is sometimes redeemed after death when his art is declared the work of a misunderstood "master." The oft-repeated myths of male-dominated art offered me nothing. H.W. Janson's *History of Art*, the most widely used art school textbook, did not include *one* female artist. (The third edition, reprinted in 1986 after Janson's death, listed eleven women artists among hundreds of male artists. The fourth edition,

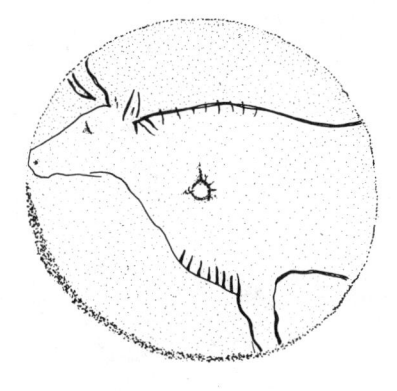

Disk with cow silhouette on one side and calf on the other. Perforated at center and probably worn as a pendant. This represents a period when animals were considered manifestations of divine power. Approximately 15,000 years old. France. (LM)

The Willendorf Goddess, originally carved in limestone and unearthed near Willendorf, Austria, is approximately 30,00 years old. She is the oldest sculpture of a human form yet uncovered. She represents the primordial Female Deity, Ancient Ancestress, who gave birth to all of Creation out of Her bountiful body. She symbolizes the abundance, bulk and stability of Earth. Original 4.5" high. Naturhistorisches Museum, Vienna.

1991, includes 29 women artists.)

I couldn't figure out how I was ever going to fit in. I was frequently told to transcend my personal experiences and develop a body of work that spoke of "universal truth." One professor actually said that using images of the Moon in art was "passé." At the same time, my own addictive and self-destructive behaviors left me physically and emotionally exhausted. I felt disconnected from my art, unable to distinguish what my advisers said I "should" do from what I really wanted to do. I was longing for relief.

When I first saw a reproduction of the Willendorf Goddess, I was stunned. She is the oldest known sculpture of a human form. My imagination was stirred by Her presence. I felt an inexplicable yet profound sense of belonging. I began researching images of women throughout ancient cultures.

My research brought me to prehistory. I was awed and fascinated by the hand-held and obviously portable Goddess figurines of the Paleolithic and Neolithic. New questions arose. What if I had grown up in an early Goddess-centered culture, honoring a Mother Goddess? How would my life be different if I were nurtured in the arms of a Wise

4 Amulets of the Goddess

Woman elder during difficult times? What would she say about art, personal experience and universal truth?

At the same time, I started reading books about shamanism, psychic healing and Goddess spirituality. The art of Mary Beth Adelson, Donna Henes, Carolee Schneeman, Betsy Damon, Nancy Azara, Audre Lorde, Harmony Hammond, and other women writers and poets inspired by Goddess images and lore, became my new role models. Lucy R. Lippard's *Overlay* and Gloria Orenstein's article "Creation and Healing: An Empowering Relationship For Women Artists" helped me re-evaluate the role of the contemporary artist in today's culture. I read Hallie Iglehart's *Womanspirit: A Guide To Women's Wisdom* and began visualizing the Goddess in meditation and prayer. I came upon the *Motherpeace Tarot* deck and used divination on a regular basis. Slowly but surely I was guided into the delicious garden of the Goddess. At long last, I was home. What I uncovered in the rich and fertile ground of the Goddess comforted my aching spirit. My life and how I perceived myself in the world changed.

So did my art. I recreated Goddess sites, filling galleries with earth and constructing places for the Goddess to enter. I cast and carved large ceramic discs that told Her story. I built Goddess temples outdoors, digging entranceways into the underground realm of Her wisdom. The titles for my art brought Her to life, healing my woman wounds: "Crying For My Mother's Mother," "Ishtar—Sky Sister,"

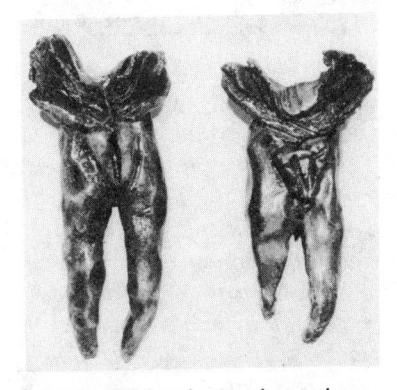

Fascinated by the Baubo, a clown-like figure who danced her lewd and bawdy gestures to restore joy and sacred sexuality to the Great Mother, Demeter, I created over a hundred clay Baubos in hopes of doing the same in my own life. I fired them using the raku process, taking each one from the kiln while molten hot and immersing it in sawdust to achieve spontaneous, unpredictable glaze and surface effects. Each one emerged from the firing a dazzling and radiant talisman.

Introduction 5

Sweet potatoes adorn an inverted pink vulva form suspended from the ceiling above several earth circles. I planted potatoes in the center and imagined the life force of the Goddess directed through the sculpture, vibrating throughout the room, touching all who entered Her "homeland." When it was completed, I realized that the potatoes reminded me of the many-breasted Artemis of Ephesus.

"Wounds That Heal, Scars That Won't," "Kali's Kiva," "Red Night, Moon Ladder," "Mother Magic," "Woman Rage," "Nest of Power." I used Goddess symbols, objects and figurines, making shrines and reliquaries. I wrote Goddess poetry. I created rituals that affirmed my female vision, voice and experience. I shut myself in my studio and meditated on the Goddess. I was having a breakthrough. *I was becoming the Goddess.*

For an entire year of graduate school I used sweet and white potatoes in all my art projects. For my thesis exhibition I filled the gallery with rich black earth and built an inverted triangular sculpture (five feet on a side) that hung from the ceiling and held 350 pounds of sweet potatoes. I made two pink neon signs that said "HOME" and placed one on each edge of the triangle. One read from the ground up, the other read from the "sky" down. In concentric earth circles below the vulva-like pendulum, I "planted" a variety of symbolic objects. In one circle I grew potatoes. In another I half-buried a dozen Willendorf Goddess sculptures that I had made, and in yet another I created little stone circles of rocks that I had gathered in my travels.

I built my own core space, reinventing my own "homeland" based on personal female experience, earth-centered spirituality and the re-awakening and returning Goddess. I created a new

When I learned how to work with neon, bending glass tubes over a large flame and illuminating them with gas and electricity, I felt like a shaman directing the forces of lightning. I had been a potter and clay sculptor for many years and working in neon seemed very similar, using the elements of earth, air, water, fire, and the ethers. This piece was inspired by a vision that I had: I was climbing a ladder filled with fragments from my past. I was required to sort through those pieces I could and could not use. Once my task was completed, I was invited to sit in a glowing "Nest of Power" where I could fly to ancient Mother Lands, growing stronger with each journey. In order to manifest the powerful healing energy of this vision, I wanted to make it real. I found a stepladder in a dumpster and wrapped it with old clothes, belts, scarves, willow branches, Willendorf Goddesses, stones and chicken bones. I then covered the entire piece with earth. I wove pussy willows into the neon nest. This piece was exhibited in the lobby of a hospital for several months.

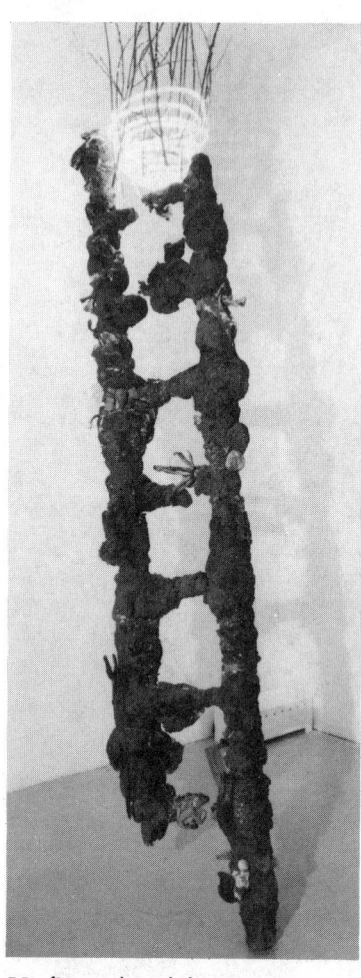

My first solo exhibition as a member of Ceres Gallery, a feminist cooperative in New York City, was titled "Kiva." I created five sculptures over ten feet tall to represent spirit guides dwelling in the womb of Mother Earth: Shark Man, Sorceress, Kali, Inanna, Root Mother. This ladder is Kali, wrapped with clothes and encrusted with earth, stones, bones and Willendorf Goddesses. The neon nest glows white.

temple or dwelling place for Her and I felt awed and centered by Her presence in the room.

As Kim Chernin says in her book *Reinventing Eve*, when you make a decision to steer away from the patriarchal path, you have to re-create your own life from a whole new set of tools and premises. My language changed. I listened carefully to the ways I perpetuated patriarchy in thought and word. I spoke up, affirming a feminist vision in my art. My relationships changed. Since my early twenties, I had been involved in one violent and abusive relationship after another. As my Goddess consciousness unfolded, I sought out caring friends and lovers who shared my awakening Goddess spirit. My eating habits changed. My body image had been so distorted that I was obsessed with dieting and losing "just another five pounds," often nearly starving myself for days. I gave up alcohol and drugs. I was embracing changes that nurtured and empowered the Goddess in my everyday life. I stopped trying to fit into anyone else's myth. From that point of transformation, the world around me began to change. And for the first time in my life I started feeling good about myself.

Contrary to what I was told in art school, art *is* healing magic.

Some ancient memory had been sparked and I knew one thing: I had to have Goddess images with me all the time. I wanted to remind myself at all times, wherever I turned, that at one time long ago, being born female was a sacred blessing and honor. I feverishly began "reproducing" Goddesses, modeling them carefully and precisely, making them as close to the original artifact as possible. I made molds and cast Goddess sculptures over and over again in clay, plaster and paper. Earth, water, fire and air: I felt like a witch, mixing magic potions and concoctions. Like a shaman, I was healing myself—healing my community. I felt like a priestess, an emissary of the Goddess. I felt like Lilith, returning to Her Motherland by the Red Sea, producing a hundred children just like Herself every day! I thought that if I could recreate *all* the ancient Goddesses, no one could ever take them away from me again.

Red Night—Moon Ladder. I became intrigued by the ladder as a symbol of shamanic healing, taking me from a disempowered place to the land of the Moon Goddess. Oil pastel.

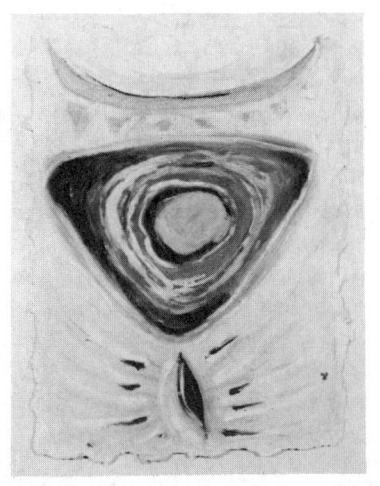

Connecting

Eager to share what I had learned, I started a women's healing group, Psychic Circle. I led workshops

Mother Magic—Horned One. Using symbols from ancient matristic cultures drew me closer to my sacred female heritage, helping me define myself in terms of herstory.

Introduction 9

on creativity and the healing process using Goddess myths and art as new models for women's wisdom and power. In 1986, one year after finishing grad school, I started Star River Productions, a mail order catalog of Goddess reproductions in sculpture and jewelry. I knew there were women and men who would want these powerful and empowering images around them, just as I did. *Star River, The Great Goddess Collection Gift Catalog* is my dream come true — a wholly integrated way of life that weaves creativity and spirituality as a source — and force — for change.

Amulets of the Goddess was born from the same passion. The actual idea for a set of Goddess Amulets came to me in a dream during intense emotional upheaval. In late 1989 I began Adult Children of Alcoholics counseling. At the same time, my business partnership was breaking up and I was planning my wedding!

During that time I had a dream in which the Goddess Lilith appeared. Her formidable presence shook me as She spoke about "radical transformation" in my personal relationships. She said I couldn't control it. She said, "Something will die. Something new will be re-born." She also said I would create something for teaching the spirituality of the Goddess. With the word "Goddess," She was gone. And I heard

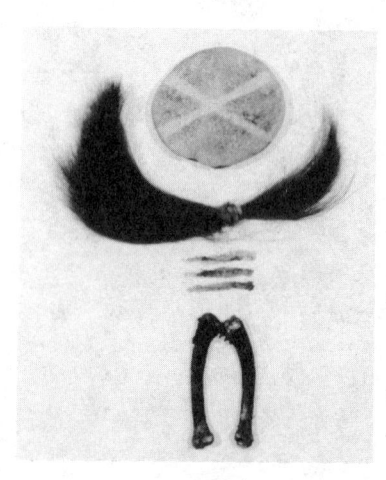

Stones, Bones and Bloodlines. Inspired by the Crown of Isis headdress worn by Egyptian queens and animal deities, I wanted to make my own symbol of personal power. I had a dream the night before I made this piece in which I was hiding from a supposed enemy. The only way out was to answer appropriately the question, What is your logo? I made this dream piece from a stone I found near a river, the ponytail from a friend's daughter's sixteenth birthday haircut, three lines of menstrual blood representing the blood mysteries of my ancestors, and gold painted chicken bones. I was trying to embrace a vegetarian diet and thought the first step would be to honor the spirit whose flesh I ate.

a cosmic crack echo through the night.

During the three-month period following the dream, Lilith appeared in daydreams and meditations, guiding my research and the creation of the Amulets, weaving together the symbology, cosmogony, art and archeology of the Goddess for use as a sacred divination tool. Whenever I needed guidance as my personal crisis unfolded, I created another disc that comforted and consoled me. For instance, as my ACOA counseling unraveled the painful memories of my childhood, I sat in meditation before beginning work on each Amulet, asking for an image that would help me understand this particular aspect of my healing process. One morning, feeling isolated and abandoned while mourning my "lost childhood," I felt the eyes of the Goddess guiding me, and I began to carve an Amulet that represented Her loving and watchful gaze. As I carved the intricate images in clay, I asked questions, and the answers flowed freely. "What do I need to remember?" "What's the best way to resolve this situation?" "How do I cope with these feelings?" When I completed sculpting the Amulets, I began interpreting the images for divinatory purposes. With my eyes closed, I chose an Amulet to guide my first words. I picked the Sa-

Lilith, Angel of the Night, is a formidable and fearless Goddess. She is known in the Hebrew tradition as Adam's first wife. She left him, refusing to be subservient to him, and returned to Her peoples of the Red Sea, a metaphor for Her reunion with the moon-worshipping cultures who honored the female blood/menstrual mysteries. She became known as the Night Owl and a Dark Goddess.

I think of winged Lilith as a strong role model for women today who need encouragement to leave unhealthy relationships. As we integrate the Dark Goddess into our lives with wise and courageous acts of power, we can feel strong and self-reliant.

The Earth Is a Goddess. As my shamanic journey to the Goddess intensified I visualized finding architectural remnants of ancient Goddess sites in my own backyard. On campus, in front of one of the engineering buildings, I created an entranceway into the center of Her "being." I made plaster molds of objects that I thought might adorn Her temples: corn, carrots, potatoes, vessels and Willendorf Goddesses. I cast them in clay and attached them to the archway and pillars. I piled a mound of rich black garden compost at the entranceway to symbolize Her navel—the beginning. Below, detail of Willendorf goddess on the pillar.

cred Animal—Frog Amulet. I listened closely to what this image wanted to tell me and what I needed to hear: "Speak up. Speak out. Express your voice. Say it the way you see it." And those were the words I wrote.

Healing

My personal journey to the Goddess is a reflection of a larger picture. As the myths, meanings and beliefs of patriarchal structures are questioned and tossed aside, we must search for new tools, patterns and models to reshape our personal lives and our global destiny. We need everyday, personal life skills. Affirmations, meditation and rituals, which develop such repressed "female" aspects as intuition and psychic awareness, must be practiced daily to eliminate the "power over" authority that has infiltrated every corner of our lives.

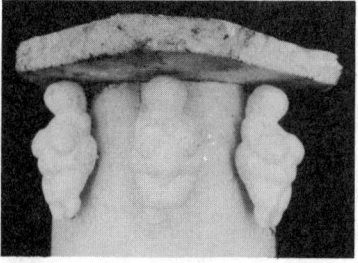

In the stories of the Goddess, we learn of peace, equality and the connectedness of all life on a sacred planet. The myth, art and artifact of ancient matristic cultures teach us that the transformative and revelatory forces of divinity are not outside us, but are immanent and within, woven throughout all personal experience. Inanna's descent to the Underworld is every woman's story, symbolic of our own psychological journey to the darkest depths of self-knowing. The Laussel Goddess holding Her crescent horn teaches the sacred mystery of our Moon time—menstruation. The ancient celebrations that link the Goddess with the seasons and cycles of Earth, Moon and Sun are deeply rooted in the psychic patterns of our lives. Everything is connected. When the Moon is full, we are affected. When species become extinct due to pollution, profit-motivated development, and overfishing or -harvesting, a piece of our future also dies. When the rain forests are destroyed, we inevitably destroy ourselves.

Goddess myths and symbols teach us that life is holy, our individual lives are valuable, and the Earth is beautiful, beneficent and sacred. We desperately need these guiding stories that can offer us hope for our future.

In solo rituals and private prayers we whisper Her name. In candlelit circles and discussion groups in kitchens, living rooms, basement meeting rooms and under moonlit skies, we gather to invoke the presence of the Goddess, calling out for Her guidance. In Goddess and Earth-centered spiritual practices we are re-learning the mythos of Great Mother as Divine Creatrix. As we do so, we challenge outmoded patriarchal beliefs, principles and precepts that have brought us exclusionary hierarchical values, violent androcratic regimes, and global desecration and destruction. Ultimately, Goddess consciousness is helping us re-imagine and re-define our own lives and the course of humanity.

The Goddess is re-emerging today as a change-maker, restoring balance, wholeness and peace by reconnecting us with Nature, our innate wisdom, and the sacredness of all life. I hope that the Amulets will guide you as they guide me, restoring female energy in our lives and ultimately in the world. They are meant to be a constant source of spiritual inspiration and practical wisdom, just as they were for our ancestors.

When you work with your Goddess Amulets, imagine that you are seeking counsel from a prophetess, ancient Goddess oracle or Wise Woman who lovingly offers support, advice and divine vision as a reflection of your own inner knowing. Active and creative use of the Amulets stimulates thoughts, memories and intuitive abilities for healing and strengthening bodies, minds and spirits. The more you use the Amulets for visualizing and contemplation, the more meaningful, potent and magical they become in personal and political transformation.

When you take the ritual of divination seriously, it will reveal its mystery to you in subtle, yet powerful ways. Ancient shamans, priestesses, witches, midwives and healers performed their magical incantations, dances and spells to connect with their Divine Sources. By the same token, each time you consult the Amulets, you are stepping into the timeless world of the Goddess for spiritual and practical nourishment.

Use your Amulets lovingly. Ponder, play and meander with the wisdom and teachings of the Goddess. Watch closely to see how Her mystery weaves itself throughout your life. Awaken to Her whisper in your dreams. Her message spoke to humanity for thousands and thousands of years. Listen, you can hear it still...

Goddess Prayer

Great Goddess,
Guide me in your wise and wondrous ways
Teach me how to live and love
In the sacred rhythms of your never-ending song.

Using Your Goddess Amulets

*She will call you
And you will know Her
Chant Her words
Sing your world alive*

Divination

When consulting your Goddess Amulets, you are participating in a divinatory ritual, which simply means that you set aside a special time to contact the divine. Divination is an ancient art, first used by our early ancestors as they closely observed nature. Changes in weather patterns and the seasonal migrations of animals determined abundance as well as danger. Early peoples mostly depended upon game, herbs, berries and wild vegetables for sustenance and survival. Understanding and cooperating with the forces of nature were necessary to assure survival. Recording the cycles of the Moon and their connection to the changes in a woman's body for information about menstruation, gestation and lactation provided a sense of continuity over time — life was not random.

Through the ages and among various cultures, divination has taken many forms. Prophets, seers, priestesses, witches, shamans and psychics have used a wide array of techniques to contact the divine, searching for meaning in the realm of the invisible. Sibyls of the Goddess babbled their visions in trance. Delphi, known as the "Womb of Creation," where Mother Earth was worshipped and consulted, was Greece's oldest oracular site. The Goddess Delphyne presided over the world's *omphalos*, umbilical of the Goddess, source of all life. Her daughter-priestesses, called Pythonesses, guarded the divination ceremonies and rites. They danced with serpents and were often bitten, and the hallucinations that the venom induced were interpreted for information. Apollo, who later presided over the Oracle at Delphi, named his oracular priestess the Delphic Bee. The buzzing of a bee was understood to be the voice of the Goddess, and a source of prophecy and divination. In many primal cultures, past and present, seeds, stones, shells, sticks and bones are tossed onto the ground and their patterns examined for answers.

As patriarchy seized power with its hierarchy and duality, male reasoning and intellect took precedence over the female psyche's intuitive, telepathic and nonrational aspects. Divination, psychic phenomena and intuitive knowledge were feared, repressed and in many cases outlawed. During the height of the Christian witch craze, women, children and men were banished, tortured and executed for using their intuitive "magic."

To reclaim the wisdom of our intuitive and psychic faculties, we must practice applying our sixth sense on a daily basis. Only then can we dispel the internalized fear that inhibits wholeness and healing.

Bee Goddess and Prophetess whose humming was the voice of the Goddess. The Delphic Oracle, Omphalos, was shaped like a beehive. Rhodes, 2,700 years old. (LM)

Ritual

Ritual is about transformation. In her book *Truth or Dare*, Starhawk says that the patterns of patriarchy are "embedded" within us. Our thoughts and emotions—our entire psyche—reflect the patterns of the death-focused and "dismembering" dominant culture around us. If we are to survive, the patriarchal myths that define humanity's past, present and future course, as well as the patriarchal mindset that defines the way we think and feel, must change.

Starhawk contends that ritual is one of the "great tools of the weavers" who help us celebrate and regenerate a "culture of life."[1]

Your Goddess Amulets are ritual tools of transformation. Each time you consult your Amulets for guidance, you dip into the well of Goddess-inspired wisdom. When you return, you bring nourishing Goddess/woman/Earth-identified values that can replace patriarchy's definitions and distortions. When you change your values, your life changes.

When I began using Goddess/woman/Earth-centered rituals, prayers and meditations, some changes manifested very quickly. My art and poetry changed dramatically. My worldview changed drastically.

Transformation that revolves around such core issues as self-esteem and self-acceptance is slow and subtle. But change that weaves itself deeply into our being is powerful and long-lasting.

Elements of ritual usually include a space, consciousness and an expressed intention or purpose. The elements of a ritual can be as simple or elaborate as you want them to be.

Ritual Space

Ritual space is where the extraordinary is to occur. It is where we create change in our lives and free ourselves from the outside world with its restrictions and male-dominated control. Altars, like rituals, prayers, affirmations and meditations, alter consciousness.

I carry my Amulets with me wherever I go, so I use a portable ritual space. I keep a ten-inch-diameter round purple silk cloth in my Amulet pouch. Silk folds easily and fits nicely into the pouch. I've stitched a few Goddess designs and sewn some colored beads on my ritual cloth, providing personal meaning to deepen the divination process. Before I consult the Amulets, I spread my cloth out before me to define my ritual space. I consciously connect the cloth and the ritual that is to follow.

By unfolding and carefully preparing my ritual space, I make the transition to my ritual mind. Preparing in a slow and attentive way shifts my awareness from "busy-ness" to sacredness, welcoming the divine energy of the Goddess into play. Ritual spaces can be very elaborate. The Goddess temples on the island of Malta in the Mediterranean and at Newgrange in Ireland are large stone megaliths that reach deep into the Earth. Their inner chambers and labyrinthine passages define sacred places where the forces of the Great Cosmic Mother were contacted and honored. Other prehistoric Goddess ritual sites include stone circles, caves, rivers, wellsprings, sacred groves, islands, mounds, and along ley lines where the Earth's energy is electromagnetically resonant.

At the Neolithic Goddess site of Çatal Huyuk in present-day Turkey a ritual space (which archeologist James Mellaart called the Red Shrine) apparently served its ancient inhabitants as a birthing room. The symbols, wall paintings, floor and furnishings were painted red. Painted figures are shown in the birth position. An altar table stood in the center of the room. Everything in the room contributed to the birth process through symbol and metaphor. We can only imagine the ceremonies that were performed there to assist the birthing mother. (See illustration, p. 111).

When I'm at home, I keep my Goddess Amulets on my altar.

Altars

An altar is a place to keep sacred objects and honor divinities. Altars can be anywhere in a room. In my bedroom, the top of my bureau is my Goddess altar where I keep sculptures, pottery, crystals, jewelry box and other Goddess-related objects. In my living room, the top of my stereo cabinet is my altar to my ancestors, with framed photos of all my family members, including pictures of myself as a child. Also included are a candle, small sculptures that represent my sacred animal guides and, whenever possible, freshly cut flowers. At work, on my "World" altar on the shelf above my sink, I keep stones and memorabilia of Goddess conferences and festivals that I've attended. When I teach work-

My Ancestor Altar: a reminder that I am part of a neverending web of life.

shops, I bring an altar cloth and create an altar on-site to focus group energy.

An altar acts as a mnemonic, an aid to memory. Every time I pass by my Goddess altar or enter my bedroom, I'm reminded that She is with me, and I am Her. When I pass my altar to my ancestors, on my way out the door in the morning, I recall that I am part of the never-ending web of life. And whenever I burn incense at my altar at work, I am reminded that I am part of a larger community of spiritual women and men who are effecting change in the world.

Create a Goddess altar. Ask yourself what you want to remember, and let that be the central issue for your sacred altar space. Then make a place for your Amulets.

Ritual Mind

When consulting your Goddess Amulets, first prepare to welcome the Divine. Many spiritual traditions call this "cleansing," and use various techniques to make the mental and physical transition into the realm of the sacred. I prefer not to use the word "cleansing." It implies that before we began the ritual we were unclean or dirty.

Before consulting my Amulets, I say the Goddess Prayer (p. 14) to move into ritual mind. Sometimes I simply take a few deep breaths to relax and to ground and center myself. You may want to invoke the presence of a Goddess who is important in your spiritual practice. For instance, I often visualize Lilith standing next to me, not only when I consult the Amulets, but also when I am facing a difficult situation. Her presence is comforting and protective to me.

Other techniques for making the transition from ordinary reality into ritual consciousness might include lighting a candle, burning incense, chanting, using rattles, drumming and movement. These are great ways to help you let go of worry and obsessive thinking and prepare for the extraordinary, intuitive, psychic and mysterious. Synchronicity is the greatest healer, weaving mystery into your daily life.

Preparing Your Amulets

The *Amulets of the Goddess* set contains twenty-seven Amulets. The number twenty-seven is divisible only by itself and multiples of three. The number three seemed a potent and magical place to begin. Each Amulet is a miniature carving of an ancient artifact. There are three groups of nine Amulets each: Great Goddesses, Sacred Animals and Sacred Symbols.

Before consulting your Goddess Amulets, spend some time familiarizing yourself with them. Touching them helps you align their energy with your own. I call this psychic bonding.

Begin by spreading the Amulets out before you. Pick them up one by one. What is your first impression? Feel the texture of the clay against your skin. Feel its weight in your hand. Rub each Amulet against your face. Explore the detail of each miniature carving. Become aware of your connection with the image.

Which ones have you seen before? What do you already know about the images? Are there some images that you are seeing for the first time? Are you intuitively drawn to a particular image? Are there images that you resist?

How do you feel? One woman has told me that whenever she begins her divination ritual, she hears the voice of her childhood Baptist minister telling her that she'll go to "hell." When she learned that Hel was the Norse Queen of the Underworld and the original Earth womb of the Goddess, she understood why Christianity reversed and perverted its meaning. Now she just smiles when she hears the word "hell" and continues her ritual of Goddess consciousness, reclaiming the magic in her life.

When you've spent sufficient time getting acquainted with your Amulets, place them in the pouch provided. Or you may have a special "power pouch" that has significant meaning for you. You may want to keep your Amulets and guidebook near your bed for morning or evening consultation. You may want to carry them with you. Wherever you decide to keep your Amulets, be mindful of their presence in your life as a tool for guidance along the sacred path, and for deepening your spiritual relationship with the Goddess within.

Consulting Your Goddess Amulets

There are several suggested readings in this chapter which offer in-depth techniques for using and consulting the Amulets. When you're ready to consult your Amulets for the first time, I recommend the single Amulet draw, called the Sacred Seed Amulet. You'll probably turn to your Goddess Amulets in this way most of the time.

When choosing a Sacred Seed Amulet, it's important to focus and clarify your intentions. You can usually express your intention as a statement that begins with the words "Great Goddess, guide me . . ." In this way, you are making clear your request for *guidance,* not answers. For instance, you might say "Great Goddess, guide me. I'm attracted to a co-worker and I'm a little nervous about having a relationship with someone I work with." Or, "Great Goddess, guide me. I'm thinking about going to Ireland for the summer." Once you make your request for guidance and state the issue or concern for which you are seeking direction, reach into the pouch. Let your fingers touch an Amulet, and pull it out of the pouch. Before reading the chapter corresponding to the Amulet, contemplate the image that you have chosen. What is your immediate impression? What are you reminded of? Resonate with the sense of the image. What does the Amulet say to you?

Each Amulet chapter is divided into three sections. The first section provides background material regarding each artifact and image, including archeological, historical, mythic and folkloric information. The background material is followed by a divinatory message that speaks to you with encouraging, loving, gentle Goddess wisdom. These messages are empowering and thought-provoking, awakening self-love, self-acceptance and the power to create healing transformation.

Following the divinatory message is a list of "correspondences" and a visualization meditation, suggested ritual or exercise for using the Amulet. The correspondences include colors, fragrances, affirmations, qualities to emulate, and a list of related Goddesses and images to gather around you for empowerment. The Correspondences act as "anchors" for fortifying your ritual work. By identifying yourself with the qualities of the Amulet image and its empowering correspondences, you strengthen and deepen your experience. Your ritual work is intensified when all your senses are engaged. When you combine drumming, music or chanting with a fragrance and visualization, you use your auditory, olfactory and visual faculties. Your gustatory (taste) sense can also be activated if you include food in your rituals. Your kinesthetic (feeling) sense is heightened when images and thoughts evoke various sensations.

Memory works by making associations. As you perform your divination ritual, using a particular Amulet image and suggested Correspondences enough times, you eventually only need touch the Amulet, smell the fragrance or see the color, and your memory of the experience will be stimulated. Ritual that includes as many senses as possible builds stronger associations, thereby creating easier access to transformation and healing. In this way, patterns of wholeness are developed.

The fragrances I've recommended are for ritual use only, not to be taken internally. If you're not attracted to the suggested fragrances, or if you're allergic to any of them, find ones that work for you. The sense of smell is highly personal. I've chosen aromas that I like. If a meditation calls for anointing your Amulet with a fragrance that you don't enjoy, the experience will not be empowering for you. An essential oil has to be pleasing to serve in ritual work. Pleasure and love are powerful healing medicine, and the basis of creative transformation.

Experiment with new fragrances for rituals and everyday use. I highly recommend the use of all-natural, pure essential oils. There are many synthetic chemical perfumes on the market. If the label does not say "pure essential oil," it is most likely synthetic. Aromatherapy, the use of essential oils for healing, is a fascinating art. Cultures all over the world have used aromatic medicines in ritual and healing rites for thousands of years. In Europe, aromatherapy is used extensively in health care practices. For further reading and research I've included books on aromatherapy in the Bibliography.

Additional Notes

All information is offered in love. The Amulets cannot cause you harm. They have no reversals or opposites. In most divination systems, whenever I pick an image in its reversed position, I immediately flip into a patriarchal mindset that says, "Uh-oh, I must be doing something wrong in my life" or "I've been bad, now I'm going to pay." Once I'm in this frame of mind, it's hard for me to hear the voice of the Divine.

The Goddess Amulet you choose comes to you as an expression of wholeness, as the Goddess Herself. I don't want to encourage patriarchal, either/or patterns and prejudices. And I certainly don't want to perpetuate the dualistic good/evil, black/white way with its fractured perceptions of Divinity. The Goddess is always "and." Each Amulet and accompanying text acts as a hologram, a seed map for revealing the whole picture, embracing all possibilities. Gentle reminders and cautions are included within the text.

How language is used in ritual, as well as in everyday life, is very important for re-patterning old behaviors and reclaiming our own authority. Most recommendations for practical magic and ritual involve dispelling "evil" or "negative" forces. "Evil" is an aspect of Christian duality, opposing an almighty "good." Evil was constructed to divide, label, persecute and oppress those whose belief systems did not conform to rigid Christian ideas of "goodness." Women, especially midwives and healers, were assigned this label, as were "feminine" men. It is still used as a manipulative and controlling tactic, instilling fear and mistrust.

I also believe that an inordinate amount of energy is focused on the so-called ubiquitous "negative forces." Words like "evil" and "negative" are usually associated with a raft of other words such as "lowly," "earthly," "blackness" and "darkness." In the hierarchical order that this comes from, women and peoples of color are grouped with evil and negativity. I prefer not to use the word "negative" as it relates to intent and purpose in ritual and magic. Several words can be used to describe unwanted or unsolicited "forces" rather than drawing on all the discriminatory, anti-female connotations inherent in words like "negative." I use words like "unkind," "unhealthy" or "fearful" to describe energies I'm dispelling. Describing them in this way helps me get a better idea of what they're really about and where they might be coming from. In this way, ritual becomes empowering, shifting the focus off some all-pervasive force "out there," bringing attention to those things that can be changed whenever possible.

Keeping A Journal

I've been keeping a journal for the past twenty years. I find that going back and reading it gives me a tremendous perspective — a map of where I've been and the enormous emotional, psychological and spiritual changes along the way. I'm able to acknowledge my progress and honor my successes. My journal helps me remember and validate my experiences — my life.

Use a journal to chart your personal growth as you consult your Amulets. In your journal, record the date you drew your Amulets and the guidance you received. Make any notes that seem relevant to the issue, especially what's going on in your life at the time. Include as many details as possible. Early on when I began journal writing I was more inclined to focus on personal issues only: feelings, moods and relationships. Now I include political and global events. When I review journal entries, I'm able to make connections on a wider scale, bridging the personal with seasonal, political and universal issues. In your journal, include sketches and doodles. Use crayons, colored pens and markers. Cut out newspaper clippings, magazine articles and images that relate to the Amulet you chose and paste them in. The more effort that you put into your journal, the more meaningful it will become as an effective "teacher." In all shamanic healing practices, the map of one's psychic journey is an essential tool!

Cleaning and Clearing Your Amulets

Many of the accompanying rituals suggest anointing your Amulets with essential oils and crushed herbs. At some point you may find it necessary to clean them. Your Amulets are made of clay, so scrubbing them lightly with a soft brush in warm, sudsy water will do. Rinse thoroughly and allow them to dry completely before using them again.

If you loan your Amulets, you may want to psychically "clear" them once they are returned to you. This means you realign your energy with the Amulets. A simple way to do this is to spread all the Amulets out before you, take a deep breath and exhale, blowing on them. Make an effort to pass over each one. Repeat the following before putting them back into the pouch: *With my sacred breath, the energy of life, I clear my Amulets and welcome them back into my hands renewed and ready to guide my journey.* This technique is also recommended after a particularly intense time, or a crisis, when all your vitality was focused on one issue and your Amulets were used repeatedly. Clearing them helps disperse accumulated energy and puts you in a frame of mind to start fresh.

Suggested Amulet Readings
Sacred Seed Draw

Seeds were sacred to Goddess communities. They guaranteed continuity and sustenance, perpetuating new growth. The simplest way to use your Goddess Amulets is by choosing a single Amulet called the Sacred Seed. There are many occasions throughout the day that might prompt you to consult your Amulets in this way. Basically, any time you feel the need for guidance in a particular situation, simply draw a Sacred Seed Amulet for an overview or a general message. In this way you're inviting the wisdom of the Goddess into your life for an added dimension to offer fresh information and stimulate new insights and perspectives.

A Sacred Seed Amulet may be used to honor special occasions: births, birthdays, anniversaries, the death of someone close to you, holidays, equinoxes, solstices, and the cross quarter days, those days that mark the midway point between equinoxes and solstices: Candlemas (February 2), May Eve (April 30), Lammas (August 2), Hallowmas (October 31).* You can also use a Sacred Seed Amulet as a theme or focus for Full Moon and New Moon ritual celebrations. For instance, in preparation for an upcoming Full Moon or New Moon festivity, the Sacred Symbol—Labrys

---

*See Z. Budapest's *The Holy Book of Women's Mysteries* for further reading on Earth's holy days.

Amulet is drawn. The Ritual of the Priestesses becomes the "theme" for the evening.

Here are suggestions for using a Sacred Seed Amulet to bring the Goddess into your life on a daily basis. You may decide to do these over the course of a week or a month, making notes in your journal and reviewing your path.

🌱 In the morning when you wake up, you stand before your altar and say the Goddess Prayer (p. 14). You choose the Sacred Symbol—Comb as an overall theme for the day. The message is Activating Self-Reliance, initiating energies of "becoming," making decisions based on your personal truth and experience. You are advised to tune in to your body wisdom throughout the day, trusting your intuitive and psychic senses. You assume the physical posture of the image on the Amulet and think about what it means to be self-reliant.

🌱 From the list of corresponding Goddesses, you are drawn to the name Shakti. You are not very familiar with this Goddess, so you take a few moments to gather more information. Barbara G. Walker's *The Woman's Encyclopedia of Myths and Secrets*, Hallie Iglehart Austen's *The Heart of the Goddess* and Patricia Monaghan's *The Book of Goddesses & Heroines* are all great resources. From *The Heart of the Goddess*, you learn that Shakti is the active life force of the universe.

🌱 You carry the Comb Amulet with you wherever you go, contemplating the Comb image, its divination message, and the Goddess Shakti. At work, you keep the Amulet in your pocket, touching it frequently. You are reminded to pay attention to your body's wise, subtle signals. At noon, you feel hungry, headachy and stressed out from pressures at work. Rather than working through lunch and grabbing a snack later on, which is what you usually do, you decide to take a break. You order a healthy take-out lunch and proceed to a nearby park. You relax while eating and take a few moments to imagine the Goddess Shakti, the life force, flowing through you, renewing your energy. You return to work feeling refreshed, your headache gone, in a better frame of mind to accomplish your work.

🍃 In the evening, you write in your journal the experiences of your day and how the Goddess Amulet helped you. How did you interpret the Amulet? What new insights were revealed to you? How did you use the information for personal growth? Before going to bed, you look at the suggested ritual at the end of the Correspondences section and decide to make a simple pendulum on the weekend as a meditation tool. You decide to invite a couple of friends so you can all make pendulums together, enjoying what Vicki Noble terms "sacred play."

A Companion Amulet

At some point you may want to draw a second Amulet as a companion to the Sacred Seed Amulet, providing clarification or confirmation on an issue. Its information may even amplify the message of the first. For example, after lunch you pull a second Amulet for clarification on the Comb Goddess. You choose the Sacred Animal—Cat, Protecting Good Fortune. During the rest of the afternoon, you imagine being surrounded by guardian Cat Goddesses, and feel relaxed in their presence, enjoying the feeling that you acquired during lunch.

Listed below are further suggestions for using the Sacred Seed Amulet in divination ritual and play.

Great Goddess Amulets

When you choose a Goddess image, use your imagination to become Her. Enact Her expression in body, spirit and emotion. Dance Her into being. Take on Her persona. How would She live out a day? How would She handle issues of conflict? How would She achieve Her goals? How would She respond to issues of global concern? How would She carry Herself? How would She feel in Her body? How would She express Her sexuality? How would She express creativity? How would She make love? How would She *be* with a friend? How would She handle death and dying? What does Her voice sound like? How would She

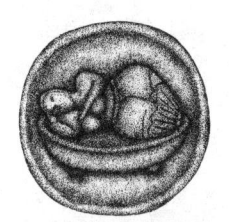

The Dreaming Goddess.

The Gorgon Goddess.

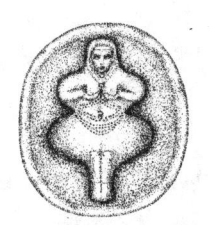

Inanna.

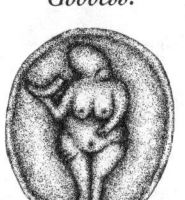

The Laussel Goddess.

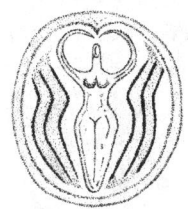

The Nile River Goddess.

The Primal Mother and Child.

The Dancing Bird Goddess.

Sheela-Na-Gig.

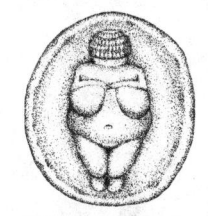

The Willendorf Goddess.

comfort and nurture a child? How would She be with Her companion animals?

Wear clothes that make you feel like Her. What fabrics would She like? Create a ritual costume for yourself that She may have worn or would joyously wear. Design an everyday Goddess outfit. Adorn yourself in Great Goddess ways. Find jewelry that reminds you of your Goddess Guide. Play with Her. Build an altar space dedicated to Her. Exchange gifts with your Guide, bringing gifts to Her altar. Gather objects you find in your everyday surroundings that remind you of the Goddess you have chosen. Create a collage of them and use it in your rituals and celebrations.

Gather images and information to learn about Her native "homeland." Use the bibliography to compile more information about the images. How does this Goddess relate to your own heritage and ancestry? Find out anything you can about embracing Her essence into your life.

Sacred Animal Amulets

When you choose a Sacred Animal image, become the spirit of the animal. Sit, stand, walk and "talk" the way your guardian animal spirit does. What strengths does your animal ally convey? In what ways can you embody Her courage? How would She nurture you? How would She protect you? How would She teach you about Her environment? What impressions does your animal guide engender in you? Do you have preconceived

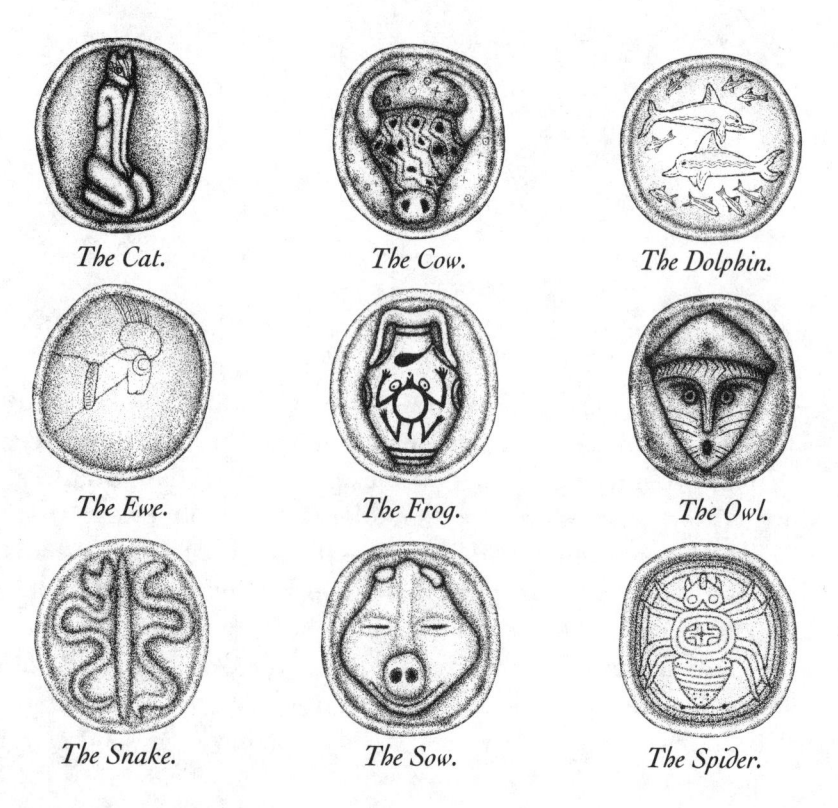

The Cat.   *The Cow.*   *The Dolphin.*

The Ewe.   *The Frog.*   *The Owl.*

The Snake.   *The Sow.*   *The Spider.*

responses or attitudes toward this animal? What among its qualities can you embody?

Create a Sacred Animal mask for ritual and celebration. (To make a papier-mâché mask, mix shredded newspaper, flour and water until they're soggy and thick. Form your mask over a rounded object. When it's dry, paint and embellish it.) Bring the magic of your animal guide into your everyday life. Familiarize yourself with animal support groups whose principles are closely aligned with your own. Use only "animal friendly" products. Find out whatever you need to know about your animal guide for empowering your spirit.

Gather animal images from other sources. What images relate? Develop a "familiar" relationship with your animal guide. Enter into a dialogue with your animal guide. Find out what wisdom your guide offers.

Sacred Symbol Amulets

When you choose a Sacred Symbol, imagine how it would feel to embody that symbol in some way. Bring it into your everyday life. Using crayons or finger paints, let the symbol be a visual mantra. Imagine, paint and invent other symbols of your own. Create a personal dictionary of sacred symbols from your experiences. Make drawings and paintings and put them up around your room.

Using body paints, paint your sacred symbol all over your body. Ask your friend to take photos of you. Make up a story about yourself as a wise and ancient healer. Use the photo of yourself to illustrate your story. Share your sacred healing story with a friend. Make a mask of papier-mâché and paint your symbol on it, attaching beads, old jewelry and whatever power objects you are drawn to. Wear your mask and tell a healing story of wise, matristic vision.

Photocopy the drawing, enlarging and reducing it many times. Place the copies everywhere around you, cutting and pasting them up where you work, on your refrigerator at home,

The Comb.   *Eyes.*   *Hand With Seeds.*

The Labrys.   *The Nightstar.*   *The Sprouting Seed.*

The Temple.   *The Triple Spiral.*   *The Whirlwinds.*

beside your bed and in your car. Make bookmarks and book covers with the image. Let the magic of the Sacred Symbol work its way into your heart. Recreate the symbol in self-hardening clay, attaching a pin back or hook so you can wear your healing symbol wherever you go. Using fabric paints, recreate the image on your clothes. Celebrate your symbols of life.

When you choose an Amulet from a particular Goddess site, fantasize living there. What might life there have been for your forebears? What would you do there? What would you wear? How would you feel in your body? What were the spiritual practices there? What was the "art" there? What images do you see being created? Using self-hardening clay, recreate some "artifacts."

Imagine how this culture might celebrate rites of passage: birth, puberty, illness, menstruation, distress, motherhood, menopause, aging, death, rebirth. How is healing approached? What talents could you offer the community? It's not necessary to have an archeological or anthropological perspective; it's actually better if you don't get caught up in being "historically correct." Invent. Recreate it in the Wise Goddess Way: gentle, simple, wise and spiritually connected to all that is. Here, the exercise of creative imagination is the practice.

Gather symbols that have meaning for you. Include symbols from past and present experiences. Imagine new symbols that help you remember the story of the Goddess.

If possible, plan a visit to a Goddess site on your next vacation.* Let yourself be drawn to a particular site by intuition or chance. Get information about Goddess Tours to specific sites. Or find a Goddess site that is associated with your ancestry, whether European, African, Asian or Native American.

Venturing to a sacred Goddess site is a very healing experience. Who would you take with you? Write about your journey while you're there so you capture your senses and emotions. Or bring a small tape recorder to record your daily experiences. And of course, bring Her back nestled deep in your soul!

However you decide to use your Goddess Amulets in the Sacred Seed draw or the more in-depth techniques that follow, you will come to love the miniature artifacts as magical talismans, poetic healing symbols and empowering mnemonic images for remembering that the guidance and loving essence of a Great Goddess are always with you. Each image opens the many cultural traditions of Goddess Spirituality. Touching and meditating on the image will create a healing space for transformation, where the Divine Female can reveal Her future wisdoms to you.

You may want to carry a particular Amulet in your pocket or power pouch for feeling close to the Great Goddess and our

---

*Two useful books on the subject are Anneli S. Rufus and Kristan Lawson, *Goddess Sites: Europe* (HarperCollins, 1990) and Natasha Peterson, *Sacred Sites: A Guide for the New Age Traveler* (Contemporary Books, 1988).

Sacred Source, Mother Earth. Perhaps you sense a connection to one of Her Sacred Animal spirits or Sacred Symbols. You may want to take the Amulet out and hold it, reconnecting with its inherent wisdom. When you embrace an image from another culture, find out about that culture. Become aware of your kinship with all others and our diverse global heritage.

Feel free to improvise and expand on the information given in the accompanying text, creating new and different ways to use your Amulets.

Dream Stone

Before going to bed, choose an Amulet for invoking Goddess dreams. Hold the Amulet in your hand or place it under your pillow. Make a wish! Or ask a question and see how it is answered in your dreams.

Journal Questions: *What wish did you make? What were you expecting or hoping the outcome would be? What Amulet did you choose? How can the Amulet help you?*

Sample Reading

A couple I know was having conflicts about money. They were caught in a round of arguments about who contributed what, who spent what, and who saved what. They loved each other dearly and didn't want this to ruin their relationship. They asked me for help. I suggested that each draw an Amulet as a Dream Stone, make a wish, sleep on it and see how it was revealed in dreams. In this way, they would have an opportunity to shift the energy from an endless loop of rationalizing and reasoning, and open to the unconscious and the unexpected.

One woman wished for a more balanced feeling about money. She received the Sheela-Na-Gig, Honoring Choices. She interpreted the Amulet and her dream to mean that she needed to establish a budget to set priorities and eliminate impulsive spending. She concluded that if she was feeling ambivalent about a purchase, she would re-evaluate it and wait until it appeared on her priority list.

The other woman wished for more trust in her approach to money. She knew that her emotions were directly connected to the balance in her checking account: When the balance was large, she felt great, but when it dipped below a certain amount, she felt insecure, even though her savings were adequate. She drew the Sacred Symbol Amulet—Sprouting Seed, New Beginnings. She interpreted it to mean that the situation was a "tender" one for her, relating to her childhood. She remembered her parents' arguing about money and the feeling that there would "never be enough" for her and her sisters. She wanted to put the past in perspective and "toss out what isn't relevant any more," as the Amulet's message suggested. She saw that she needed to cultivate trust, that she could take care of herself, and that the Universe was based not on scarcity but abundance.

My friends shared their dreams and wishes, coming to a better understanding of each other's attitude toward money and how it affected their relationship. They established a "fun account" to which they made small but equal weekly contributions, using it for weekend "play" activities. The "fun account" helped to defuse the seriousness around the issue.

Ritual of the Elements

The Earth, the Water, the Fire, the Air
Return, Return, Return, Return

The natural elements of Earth, Water, Fire and Air influence our lives with their profound energies. They represent all that was, is and will be. And they are the essential elements of our own bodies. In spiritual traditions the world over, the Great Goddess created the elements and saw fit to distribute and administer their powers.

The number four has determined universal and human structure throughout the ages: the four phases of the menstrual cycle;

the four seasons; the four cardinal points; and the "four corners of the world."

Invoking the elements and calling forth your Goddess Guides is a profound ritual and meditation. By choosing an Amulet to coincide with each element, you are calling forth a Goddess Guide for helping you acknowledge, embrace and empower the universal elements in your life. Integrating the elements into your life in healthy, nurturing ways helps you live closely in tune with the Earth.

Mary Daly stirs a passionate feminist voice about women and the Elements. She says that the various metaphors associated with the elements actually comprise "deep Realms of reality with which our senses are naturally and Wildly connected."[2] Remembering and honoring Elemental spirits is a must for women's empowerment, conjuring memories of "Archaic integrity" that phallocentric philosophies and religions have limited and broken.

To begin the ritual of the elements, create a sacred space that has power and meaning for you. Bring your journal. Before choosing your Elemental Amulets, place four small bowls in a circle, each bowl corresponding to an element. In one, place some Earth. In the next, place some salt Water. In the next, a candle for Fire. Leave the last bowl empty for Air. If you are inclined to incorporate the four directions, you might want to place Earth in the North, Water in the South, Fire in the West and Air in the East. Honor what feels comfortable for you. You may want to choose an Amulet to symbolize the additional three directions: Sky (above), Earth (below), Center (heart). Light the candle. Choose an Amulet for each element, placing it beside each corresponding bowl. For each element consider the following:

Earth Earth is Gaia, Mother, all that we are and more, all that we stand on. We are alive only because She provides for us from Her body. Every living creature is Her beauty and bounty and is essential to our survival. We are infected with the patriarchal disease of forgetting. The cure is remembering our Earth Source, using the resources that Earth provides us in partnership and cooperation, recycling and returning them to Earth in appropriate ways so they can be renewed and regenerated. This is the contract of our bond to Earth.

The element Earth is our relationship with our own mother, whose body was the source of our birth. We remember the story of our mothers and our mothers' mothers. In our growing awareness, we understand the consequences on the lives of all women who have lived in a male-dominated culture. We are also called upon to put together the pieces of our lost matristic heritage, a body of information that can replace the emptiness in our souls, and ultimately restore our vision for a peaceful, egalitarian future on Earth.

In our bodies, the element Earth is our flesh and bones, forming the sacred "temple." By invoking the element Earth we take care of our bodies and nourish our only true "home." Food is thus spiritual nourishment for every cell. This requires that we honor and love our bodies. (Beware: Transcendent spiritual practices promote physical purification and detoxification to "get out of the body." This is just another form of body hatred!)

How are you nurturing your body? Listen closely to the inherent wisdom of physical, emotional and spiritual distress signals that provide information for well-being. In the Wise Woman Tradition, healing is always an act of love.* Body hatred and denial run rampant in our culture, leading to addictive behaviors that jack us up and bring us down. Distractions and addictions come in many forms and take us out of our bodies, our lives, and our painful, personal stories.

If your body is trying to tell you something, use your Goddess Guide to get in touch with its message. Take a journey with your Goddess Guide into the center of your body. What does your body want to say about the story of your life? Tell your story to

---

*For further information on the Wise Woman Tradition of healing, see Susun Weed's *Healing Wise*. I also recommend Stephanie Demetrakopoulos' *Listening To Our Bodies: The Rebirth of Feminine Wisdom*. And particularly helpful in this area is *Focusing*, by Eugene Gendlin.

your Goddess Guide. Let Her hold you and listen to you. Honor all that your body has provided for you.

The element Earth is always BODY. Whatever Amulet you have chosen for this element will help you remember your relationship to the great bodies of wisdom: Earth, Mother, Self. Take time to envision and enact partnership, care and cooperation with each.

Gather images of Earth and Earth elements all around you. Practice the most powerful political act of all time: Love the body you have. Healing unfolds quickly in the hands of tender loving care. Make notes in your journal of personal acts of power regarding your body. Carry along your Goddess Guide for the element Earth to remind you of where you live and help you take an environmental stand.

Water The element Water is moving and magical, life's essence. Without water nothing grows. Goddess-worshipping cultures celebrated lifegiving moisture from Her body by creating images of Her eyes, vulva and breasts in sculpture and decoration. Her womb was the vessel that contained the liquid in which all things grew. Her rivers, oceans and lakes provided a place for early cultures to create their communities. And each body of water offered abundant nourishment so Her children could flourish and grow.

Today we are suffering elemental amnesia, or what Gloria Orenstein calls "eco-amnesia."[3] We have forgotten our connection to the natural world. Earth's waters have been polluted by the patriarchal poisons of domination, control, violence and greed. And women of the world have been sucked dry. We need to remember our responsibility to protect our water sources and our woman-sources. Women are reclaiming strength and courage in images of the Divine Female. Imagine a loving and intimate relationship with Water.

In our own bodies, this element comprises our tears, blood and sweat; it is the salty solution of a mother's womb, and mirrors the depths of our emotions. A Goddess Guide for Water will help you re-establish "the flow." You will also be amazed at the healing power of a vigorous, sweaty walk.

If you are unblocking stoppages from physical, emotional or sexual abuse, find comfort in soothing warm herbal baths, the release of memories in tears, and ritual visits to rivers, lakes, and the sea. A ritual that I often suggest to students who are facing an emotional crisis is one I call Ocean Rites. I first did this while visiting friends in Cape Cod. They invited me to help them perform a healing ritual about a rape incident involving a classmate at school. We walked to the ocean, gathered dried seaweed on the beach, and made a seaweed spiral twenty feet across. We gathered in the middle of the spiral, holding hands and facing the ocean. One by one we asked the Great Mother Ocean to soothe our hurt, speaking openly about personal experience of violence and abuse. In single file we "unwound" out of the spiral, finding a comfortable place in the sand near the water's edge to create symbols of the emotional hurt that we wanted healed. Each of us worked in silence, letting the whispering sound of the water comfort us. After we finished, we stood arm in arm chanting, waiting and watching as the waves eventually washed away our "pain."

Menstrual rituals for reclaiming our birth and blood rites/rights also stimulate the flow of Divine restorative energies. The underlying healing quality of Water and the part it plays in the body encourage natural and rhythmic movement.

Gather images of water and water beings for nurturing your feelings. Carry your Goddess Guide with you as a reminder of the element Water. Melt away restrictive anti-living, anti-feeling, anti-being rulers. Undulate in free-floating, meandering rhythms.

Fire The element Fire is the spark of life: the Sun, the stars, lightning, the warmth from a hearth's flames and the glow of love in our hearts. Fire represents the dynamic energy of continual renewal and transition. It is the element that breaks down in order to build back up.

Fire is our physical energy, our passion and our creativity.

Athletes call it the "fire power" of the nervous system that ignites concentrated and intense physical performance. Fire is always associated with female sexuality.

When you choose a Guide for the element Fire you spark shamanic healing. According to Vicki Noble, shamans have always been the "Magicians of Fire," dancing the spirit of lightning back into the spiritually wounded.[4]

If you feel "burned out," you may be too close to the Fire. If you're dispassionate or lack the energy to stimulate transition in your life, then you're sitting too far from the hearth. Slide closer to the Fire to get charged up! (Adrenaline rushes of the addictive kind are not the nature of this element. Addictions destroy the life force.)

Gather images of the Sun, Moon and Stars. Wear fiery colors like reds, oranges and golden yellows. Find ways of transforming anger for creating change. Get in touch with your sensual self.

(I'm always compelled to lecture on the difference between eroticism and pornography when I get into the nature of sexuality. If the arousal of sexual response requires the deadening of feeling, this fact does not belong to the nature of sexuality. It is the nature of sexuality to arouse feeling, and of feeling to arouse sexuality. Susan Griffin makes a clear distinction: Human erotic feeling is "a love of the life of the body;" Eros is "our own wholeness...the whole experience of human love." The capacity to fully enjoy our sexuality is a return to healing and wholeness. Pornography is "the fear of bodily knowledge" and an attempt to silence, repress or distort Eros.[5])

Get to know the energy of arousal without the need to "do" something with it. Let your Goddess Guide whisper words of erotic passion in your ear. Feel the glow of your sexual energy. Know what makes you feel sexually alive in your body. Acknowledge your creative energy. Create something from scratch. Find a mentor for igniting change. Find a group whose values give form to healing and transition. Get out of lukewarm apathy. Stretch yourself into the element Fire. Your Goddess Guide will teach you to dance with Fire.

Air Air is the element that stirs up life, the invisible made visible in the realm of motion. Air is Sky, the breath of Earth. It is the natural, transformative energy of whirlwinds, zephyrs, hurricanes and tornadoes.

Air feeds Fire, absorbs Water and carries Earth. It is the the renewing breath of Spring and the freezing gales of Winter.

Air is breath, nourishing our bodies' cells. It is the medium that carries sound so our voices and stories can be heard.

When choosing your Goddess Guide for help in honoring and invoking the element Air, think about how you breathe. Do you give yourself fresh air for new thoughts? Are your breaths deep and strong, slow, gentle and long? Do you remember to breathe during emotional upsets? Do you know the rhythm of your own breath? Does your voice communicate from your heart? Do you voice your opinions? Do you hold yourself back, afraid to speak your mind? Do you waste your breath in conversations that go nowhere? Do you speak the language of coercion and manipulation? What do you really want to say, and to whom?

Do you have a sense of the space you take up? Are you comfortable in your space? Do you find yourself apologizing for taking up space? Do you have enough space? Do you have a space of your own? Do you need to create one? Do you have a sense of your boundaries and those of others? Are there people in your space who are not welcome? Do you want to welcome new relationships into your space? Let your Goddess Guide help you find answers for incorporating the element Air in your life.

Gather images of this element for your journal. Winged creatures, sky, clouds and movement all relate to Air. Air is also the element that encourages chanting and singing. Learn new songs for expressing your heart and soul.

Sample Reading

When invoking your *Elemental Goddess Guides*, keep in mind that they are in an inseparable continuum. Once you have chosen four Guides, each corresponding to an element, take a close look at them. A Goddess will offer comfort, wisdom and a harmonious relationship with that element. For instance, choosing the Willendorf Goddess (which symbolizes the bounty of Mother Earth and the ecstatic sense of belonging) for the element Water can help you improve your emotional expression, encouraging you to reap the bounty of your emotional being.

The Sacred Symbol—Goddess Temple, Breakthrough, Awakening Healing connected with Water might suggest that you incorporate Water in healing rituals and visualizations. You may interpret it to mean that you need to drink more water for better health!

Choosing the Sacred Animal—Dolphin Amulet, Joy for Fire may be telling you to take time to enjoy your sexuality, creativity and heightened energy.

With the four Elemental Amulets in front of you, imagine asking each Guide for help integrating the elements in your life and body. Trust whatever messages or images come up for you, even if they don't make sense. Make notes and drawings in your journal. Later on, review your experiences and make additional notes that relate to the outcome of the Ritual of the Elements.

Consider creating an Elemental Power Bundle. Wrap your four Amulets in a piece of cloth that has meaning for you. Write an affirmation and include it in the bundle. Carry the bundle with you and remember the images throughout the day, taking them out when you want to "touch home." Trust your elemental being.

The Triple Goddess

The Trinity of the Goddess embodies the three most powerful passages of a woman's life, celebrated as "blood mysteries" from ancient matristic cultures the world over. The Maiden aspect of the Trinity is when a young girl lives in her dreams, for herself; her imagination is the playground of infinite possibilities and fantasy. A girl's menarche signals her connection to the rhythms of the Moon and her awakening to the Mother feature of the Trinity. In her sacred Mother power, she creates the world.

Creative expression, personal achievement, childbirth, sharing, and caring are all ways of tapping into "motherhood." Her essence is fulfillment as she begins to realize the dreams of her child self. The Crone phase of the Triple Goddess, when a woman's wise blood remains within, is a time of great dignity and power. She teaches from her life's experience as shaman, elder, aunt, healer and grandmother. Her wisdom weaves the mystery of death and rebirth back into life.

The Goddess and Her priestesses presided over all three of these domains in early matristic societies. Each point of the Trinity had a guardian Goddess administering the rituals of that passage. The Greeks called the Triple Goddess Hebe-Hera-Hecate. In Ireland She was the Morrigan, Ana-Babd-Macha. Kali is India's Triple Goddess, called Parvati-Durga-Uma. The three Gorgons were Sthenno-Euryale-Medusa. The Vikings had the three Norns, the Romans had the triple Fates or Fortunae, and the Druids called Her Diana Triformis.[6] The Triple Goddess is Morning-Noon-Night. I also refer to the Trinity as Daughter-Mother-Grandmother. The Trinity of the Goddess is the Great Round — She who embraces All.

The Triple Goddess helps me remember that all things have a beginning, a middle and an end — but not necesarily in that order. The Three help define boundaries and limitations, providing a bal-

Celtic Triple Goddess. In this image one Goddess holds an infant in swaddling cloth, the middle Goddess holds a scroll and the third holds what appears to be bread or perhaps a small percussion instrument. All three offer their right breast as a gesture of nurturance. They may represent Mother-Midwife-Shaman as well as Mother-Maiden-Crone. They affirm an overall matristic theme: women create. When I recreated this sculpture I was drawn to the undulating rhythm that connects their arms, hands, clothing, and hair. They seem woven together — a vibrating tapestry of life. Approximately 2,100 years old. France.

anced perspective on the life process. I imagine each Goddess of the Trinity making love with Time in a majestic and beautiful dance of life. Each relinquishes Her reign as the next Goddess steps out on the dance floor, sharing an eternal moment of ecstasy.

Choose an Amulet to help guide you or someone you know through the rites and passages of the Triple Goddess. Before selecting an Amulet, you may want to create a sacred space around you by lighting a candle, chanting, dancing or practicing creative visualization. Use your journal for making notes. As always, the appropriate Amulet will appear.

Maiden Amulet, Menarche/First Blood

When an Amulet is chosen for a girl's first blood, the image on this, her *Blood Stone*, becomes an invaluable guide, counselor and companion throughout her life. A ceremony might revolve around her embracing this image as a Goddess Guide during this passage into womanhood. Drawings, stories, songs, guided meditations and related images of the Amulet chosen provide a focal point for a menarche ritual. This may include making a mask, a costume or several body adornments that relate to the image of the *Blood Stone*.

Her grandmother, mother, older sister, aunt or Wise Woman friend may fashion a power bundle or pouch decorated with the design from her chosen *Blood Stone* as a symbol of her welcome into

Daughter of the Sea, Young Aphrodite represents the time when a young girl lives in her dreams, her imagination and her fantasies. She represents unlimited potential—being and becoming. Her beauty is reflected in all of life. Approximately 2,300 years old. Greece.

the "family of Wise Women." Her father, brother or uncle may want to share a story of female courage, strength, achievement and empowerment within the Goddess traditions that relates to her *Blood Stone*.

Her first menstrual calendar can include images of Goddesses, Sacred Animals and symbols. Her first journal may display the likeness of her *Blood Stone*. All of these help her embrace and honor her own sacred blood rhythm and womanhood.

A *Blood Stone* can be chosen by women who want to reclaim the power of their menstrual cycle at any time in their lives.

Mother Amulet, Ovulation/Menstruation/ Honoring Life's Flow

A *Blood Stone* picked during ovulation and menstruation helps reclaim the sacredness of the cycle. Becoming aware of the complex physical, emotional and spiritual changes that occur during these times can help overcome patriarchal menstrual taboos and put a woman's fragmented rhythm back together for health and well-being.

Menstrual rituals might be simple, personal "acts of power" or more complex ceremonies involving other women. The image may be recreated in drawings, stories or songs for remembering the profound and mysterious wonder of this special time. Carry your personal *Blood Stone* in your power pouch or in a pocket to be

Menstruating woman as cosmic flow-er. 18th century wood carving, South India. (LM)

touched, and call upon your Goddess Guide for comfort and counsel.

A *Blood Stone* can be held tightly and squeezed during difficult menstrual cramping, easing tension. In many ancient cultures, menstruation was when women left the village, disconnecting from everyday routine and opening to heightened psychic abilities. If you use it as a mandala, a *Blood Stone* can be the entry point for a meditative trance in which you experience visions, dreams and wisdom. Listen deeply to your Goddess Guide during this sacred blood time.

Crone Amulet, Menopause/Wise Woman Blood

At the onset of menopause, when a woman's wise blood is retained within, a *Blood Stone* marks the transition to her new energies and the community of Wise Elders and Crones. Croning, Queening or Elder rituals can make use of the image on the chosen *Blood Stone* for mask-making, dance and story.

A Crone can embellish a costume or cape with Goddess designs taken from her *Blood Stone* and create her personal Power Belt for this magical post-menstrual time. A newly initiated Crone may select a *Blood Stone* as a guide for the adventures to occur in her age of wisdom, or she may want to start her Crone Journal, writing her life stories, experiences and dreams, using images of her Goddess Guides throughout.

This crowned Snake Goddess from ancient Crete symbolized the guiding spirit of the Crone: Woman of Age, Woman of Wisdom. The Crone-becoming-Shaman sits in meditation calling forth Her oracular visions. Approximately 8,000 years old. Crete. (LM)

46 *Amulets of the Goddess*

Whatever Amulet is chosen, recreate the image to invoke Goddess guidance for the Crone Way. Break the menopause taboo by summoning a Crone Circle so that you can be with other women making this blood rite of passage in their lives. Choose *Blood Stones* as "topics" for sharing anecdotes and personal reminiscences. Get in touch with empowering tales of courageous Crones. Speak the unspeakable, think the unimaginable.

Sample Reading

A friend who was going through menopause asked me for suggestions on doing a Croning Ritual. She wanted to do something meaningful that related to her personal experiences. I suggested she consult the Amulets. She chose the Sacred Symbol — Nightstar Amulet, Fulfillment. She laughed and interpreted the Amulet to mean that now was the perfect time to ask for something she had always wanted.

She decided that she wanted a Croning Ritual on the beach. She was born in Maine and had fond memories of summers when her family visited her grandparents by the shore. She also needed to heal the emotional wound of a sexual abuse incident that she had suffered there. So she planned her Croning celebration for a late summer afternoon on the beach. She invited her closest friends, asking them to share a song, a poem or a small gift to help her heal the past and embrace the future in joy, love and wisdom. She sewed a Crone Cape for her special day, made of deep purple velvet. She said it reminded her of the night sky in Maine. Using the Nightstar Amulet as inspiration, she embroidered three silver stars on the inside of her cape, symbolizing the Trinity of the Goddess. She embroidered a red circle around the third star — the Crone.

At the beach, she sat radiantly poised for the ritual in her purple Crone Cape. A close friend crowned her with a tiara made of purple iris and white roses woven together with thyme, mugwort and sage. Everyone sat in a circle around her and as each gift was presented, we all chanted, "Wise Woman, Wise

Woman, let your power unfold; Wise Woman, Wise Woman, let your story be told." After the giftgiving, she related her story about the sexual abuse incident. When she finished, she walked around the circle and received hugs from everyone. Just before sundown, we shared a potluck dinner. The ritual ended with everyone lying on a blanket, heads together, pointing to stars and making wishes for our Crone friend's future.

Journey Amulet

A *Journey* Amulet provides Goddess guidance for travel. It may also serve as an element for a ritual or celebration involving the intent or purpose of the journey. Carry your Journey Stone with you and call on your Goddess Guide. In your journal, write about your feelings prior to, during and after your trip. Make note of any unusual, coincidental or spontaneous instances that occurred, paying attention to senses, smells and details. How did your Guide help you on your journey? What rituals did you enact while there?

After my first year in graduate school and my introduction to the Goddess, Leo (whom I had met in school and would eventually marry) and I decided to take a trip together. We knew without hesitation that we wanted to go to England.

But once there, after a few days of seeing castles and war memorials, I grew frustrated with the imperial monuments to death and killing. We rented a car and visited sites to which we felt intuitively drawn. We came upon several mounds, stone circles, and little known and sparsely attended Celtic sites. While driving along one road we knew we were in the area of Stonehenge but weren't sure where it was. Suddenly we saw the magnificent ring of giant stones in the distance. Immediately tears welled up in my eyes. The awesome "presence" of my ancestors pulsed in my veins. Our five days in the pagan British countryside brought me closer to my ancient heritage.

When we returned, we visited a "seer" who told us that in a past life, Leo and I had lived together in Britain and worked as farmers to gain passage to America on a boat. Prior to going into trance, we told her nothing of our trip!

Consider choosing an Amulet for the following journeys:

- Traveling to a sacred place on Earth.
- Returning to the place of your birth.
- Visiting friends or family.
- Making a pilgrimage to a sacred Goddess site.
- Visiting the grave of a deceased family member.
- Going to the place of your ancestors.
- Returning to a place where you used to live.
- Journeying to where you want to live.

Sample Reading

After two and a half years of Adult Children of Alcoholic counseling, I wanted to have a memorial gathering at my father's gravesite. He had been dead for fifteen years and I felt the need to heal old wounds. I invited my three older brothers and their families to participate.

I felt very anxious about the upcoming event since my brothers and I rarely talked about our childhoods. Like good ACOA's, we tenaciously guarded our secrets. I was also a little nervous about their response to a ritual gathering. This would be new for them. I consulted my Goddess Amulets for guidance. I received the Sacred Animal—Cow, Uniting In Partnership. I interpreted it to mean that the timing was propitious for me to join with my family, speak from my heart, and author my own script—life was not a performance for someone else. I sent out invitations, outlining the ceremony as a time to honor our feelings and release the past, asking those who wanted to share a story, a reading, a gift. Our family holiday gathering was scheduled for December 21, 1991, and we decided to do the memorial at the same time. December 21 was a Full Moon, a partial lunar eclipse and the day before Winter Solstice! I imagined Hathor, the Great Horned Cow Goddess, smiling at me from Her celestial abode. I had spoken to my brothers on the phone before leaving and I sensed tension about the upcoming event. Before driving to New England I slipped the Cow Amulet into my pocket. The Great Moon Goddess by my side, I felt comforted.

When I arrived, we all crowded into my brother's station wagon and rode to the gravesite. The conversation on the way was strained. I rubbed the Cow Amulet in my pocket over and over. I brought a plain pine wreath with me. The ground was snow-covered. We all held hands in a semicircle facing the gravestone. I began the ritual by drawing a heart in the snow and placing the wreath over it. My oldest brother read a passage from a book that talked about beginning one's childhood at any time. My other two brothers acknowledged "the tough times" and the need to remember the good ones. Not knowing what to expect from them, I was quite flabbergasted. When it came my turn to speak, I talked about my anger, my lost childhood, and the years of silence. I felt a little embarrassed about crying in front of my big brothers, but let the tears flow anyway, releasing my feelings into the cold Connecticut sky. My brother squeezed my hand in his, and I finished what I needed to say, feeling supported and loved. I thought about Nut, arching over us, protecting me, guiding me on my healing journey.

When everyone finished speaking, we tenderly hugged. I could feel an enormous sense of relief. Before leaving the gravesite, I saw the edge of an orange Moon rising over the trees. My oldest brother looked at me as I pointed to the Moon in silence. "That's powerful stuff, isn't it, Nance?" I just smiled. In the car, on the way back to my brother's house, we agreed to return each year to my father's gravesite for a memorial gathering.

Amulet of Well-Being

You may pick an Amulet of Well-Being during times of illness and periods of recuperation. A Goddess Guide can be your companion and ally for resting and renewing vital energy. Make an Amulet part of a simple healing ritual. Wrapping and winding thread, yarn, string, cloth or wire around sticks, rocks or power objects while you repeat healing mantras help focus attention when you are "binding healing energy." Keep your healing mantra simple. The one that I often use is: "I heal myself in love." Remember that during the healing process you are called back to the "well" for your journey into the watery womb of the Great Mother. While there, avoid the Inquisition of the Why's: Why am I sick? Why didn't I do this or that? Why me? Why now? Also, avoid the Lesson Trap. Trying to "learn lessons" from illness can bring on the biggest case of the guilts you'll ever see. The Lesson Trap triggers the compulsion to "figure it out" and "get it right," subjecting you to increased stress. In the Wise Woman tradition, illness is a time for unconditional, loving, tender care and nourishment, allowing the healing process to unfold.

Journal Questions: *During these underworld "dips into darkness," nurture and love every part of yourself. How can you ally your illness or disease? Listen to the simple, profound wisdom of your body. Healing is a loving process on the great spiral of awakening self-love.*

Sample Reading

Recently I felt the early symptoms of a sore throat coming on. For me, this is always a message to stop "doing" and take time out for renewing. I took the afternoon off work, crawled into bed and drew the Gorgon Goddess Amulet, Transforming Anger. This message was very appropriate because I had been reluctant to communicate my frustration and anger about an annoying situation in my office building.

I gathered my box of found objects and artmaking materials around me on the bed and decided to transform my anger into a focus on healing. I found a large spool of red yarn that I had picked up at a rummage sale and a smooth flat stone that I had brought home from a beach in Nova Scotia. I let my intuition guide me as I began wrapping the red yarn around the stone. I visualized myself saying what I needed to say regarding the situation at work. As the image became clearer, I started to say the words out loud. I continued to wrap the yarn around the stone, binding the energy of my words to the image of myself speaking up at work. I kept the Gorgon Amulet in front of me and occasionally imitated the expression on Her face. When I finished, I held the yarn-wrapped stone in one hand and the Gorgon Amulet in the other as I dozed off to sleep. I awoke in time for dinner, feeling much better. I also felt fully prepared to face the situation that I was avoiding at work. Today, my healing red stone sits on my altar as a reminder to love my anger as expansive and transformative energy.

The Great Goddess Council

You may choose to do the Great Goddess Council reading when you are facing an emotionally intense issue. Having four members of a wise council guide you offers a variety of different outcomes, deepening the meaning for you.

Imagine that you are calling a meeting of the Wise Woman clan elders to share your story. The Great Goddess Council is the gathering of the Crones: the shamans, the witches, the priestesses who heal with compassion, loving kindness and honesty. You are calling them today to guide you on your journey. You are seated before them—and with them. They have witnessed the seasons and cycles, rhythms and patterns of many lunations. Their ancient wisdom comes from the heart of the Goddess Way. Each Goddess Guide will offer you a gift for healing and guidance.

Priestesses/shamans performing snake dance. Clay sculpture, approximately 3,500 years old. Crete. (LM)

Before choosing the four Amulets that will comprise the members of your Great Goddess Council, imagine the excitement of a meeting with the elders. Imagine a circle of Wise Women of which you are a member. Imagine a place of comfort and understanding.

Imagine sharing your story in sacred song and ritual as they listen carefully to you. Imagine them drumming and rattling, calling you into the circle, their arms outstretched, waiting for you.

When you're ready, prepare your question, your issue at hand. Then choose four Amulets and place them before you. Ask the Council your question. Before reading the text accompanying the Amulets, resonate with each one; what do you intuitively think the response or comments would be?

Use your journal for writing and marking the events of your meeting. This is important for keeping in touch with your Goddess Guides and for remembering their offerings. Record the date that you called together the Great Goddess Council and indicate the issue you presented. Make a list of the Amulets that you drew. How did you interpret the divination message of each? Describe how you feel and its meaning for you. Keeping a journal will help you see changes and transformations on your journey.

When you consult the Wise Woman Council, imagine standing before them and with them, as this drawing indicates. You are participating in a shamanic healing ritual in which you hold the power of the snake — regeneration and renewal — in your hands. (LM)

Sample Reading

A friend wanted advice about her complex personal situation, involving a new love interest and a relationship she was just getting out of. She felt overwhelmed and confused. We decided to call a meeting of the Great Goddess Council. She first presented her situation: "I'm calling together the Great Goddess Council to help me remember what I need to know about the situation I'm in." She then chose four Amulets:

Sacred Symbol — Whirlwinds, Trusting the Invisible
The Nile River Goddess — Strength, Triumph, Success

Sacred Animal — Dolphin, Joy
Sacred Symbol — Labrys, Accepting Priestess Power

She sat contemplating the images. She felt as if she was the little figure in the middle of the whirlwinds and really wanted to dance and swim like the dolphins. The Nile Goddess seemed to be telling her to "stretch" a little and move out of her physical and emotional comfort zone in order to get a fresher perspective. And the labrys seemed comforting to her, instilling a sense of balance. She read the accompanying text and resonated with each message.

Taking a deep breath, she realized that she really needed to trust her feelings and learn how to establish healthy boundaries. She also felt the need to embrace humor in the midst of chaos. The order in which she received the Amulets seemed significant to her, revealing the process from confusion to empowerment. Later, she decided to practice the "In the Whirlwinds" meditation (p. 177) since she drew this image first and felt intuitively drawn to it.

The Spiral Journey

In this process, you draw seven Amulets from the pouch and place them in a spiral. The spiral is a symbol or map for one's life journey, beginning in the center, the realm of darkness and completion, and expanding outward. In her book *Healing Wise*, Susun Weed makes a clear distinction between the healing process as it is perceived on the Heroic (Patriarchal) Spiral and on the Wise Woman Spiral:

> Heroic Spiral:
> My life from the view of the Heroic tradition begins when my soul slips from perfection and falls into form. Immaculately conceived as a cosmic circle/egg of completeness, I should be able to continue on endlessly in perfect balance.

But I am born in sin. My body and mind are not to be trusted. So when I follow the Heroic tradition, I put my hope in following the rules.

The rules help me keep clean and clear. When I break the rules I get punished: get sick, break a leg, lose my sweetheart, get a traffic ticket. I try to learn my lessons, the teachings of my pain, so I'll never have to experience bad things again ... entropy quietly takes a bit of my vitality as I go round the spiral and this alone slowly unwinds me into death, unclean death. Trying to outwit death with rigorous cleansing measures, I move my spiral more rapidly inward.... The more rigidly I adhere to the rules, the less flexibility I have and the less vitality flows through me... I constrict the space of my self-love ... Thus, the spiral turns in, quickly in to unruly death's realm—failure.[7]

Wise Woman Spiral:
I begin at the center, says the wise woman seer. I come from the chaos and the completeness at the center of the spiral.

I am vital, moving, growing, unrestricted in resources.... In the natural flow of my expansion and enrichment, I encounter pain; I lose control; I die. In the natural flow of my curiosity and play, I discover joy and wisdom. I am born. Pain is inevitable, suffering optional in the Wise Woman tradition.

When I hurt (when my heart hurts, when my head hurts, when my shoulders hurt) I nourish my heart, my head, and my shoulders. I am strengthened, transformed and deepened ...

I expand. I open my spiral. I ask myself, "How can I make this problem my ally? What is the gift of health / wholeness / holiness here?" I gain energy with each sickness or problem. My range of resonance and my capacity to receive and to share increases every time I

Using Your Goddess Amulets 55

encounter pain and loss and make it my ally. I ally myself with all that I resist and thus become whole. I regain my holiness. Every time I nourish myself in pain, honor my distress, and love my uniqueness, my vibration is vitalized and the spiral gets bigger and more open . . .

My every disease a transformation . . .

Yes, death is part of my whole self. I expand, compassionate, confident, successful. I let loose, flying off into death, birth, void, full. . . . I become completion. I am one with the beloved again! She died laughing. She died in ecstasy. She died with her eyes wide open.[8]

As you spiral on your journey, drawing an Amulet for each step, your Goddess Guide will ask you to honor seven aspects of yourself. Each step includes all possibilities. For instance, the first Amulet represents your gifts and talents. If they are denied, repressed or unrealized, they can be experienced as a burden. Remember that the Goddess Way is always "and," embracing the All and the Nothing. You may choose to take only one step and stay with it until you feel comfortable taking the next step, or you can enter the spiral at the place that calls you. It isn't necessary to begin at the beginning. You may decide to pace yourself, taking a week, a month or a year to complete the journey. Do it in a way that feels comfortable for you. Your journey will bring you to the place you need to be, eventually embracing the whole picture.

Prepare yourself. The Spiral Journey is a ritual of healing transformation. Give yourself a period when you won't be disturbed. You may want to take the Spiral Journey with a friend or in a group, each taking a turn choosing an Amulet and sharing her story. Or

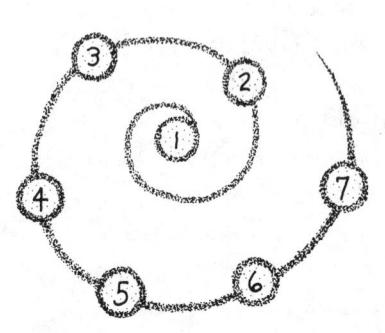

Choose seven Amulets, one at a time, beginning with the center, the heart of the Goddess. (LM)

you may use the Spiral Journey within the context of your therapy or counseling, adding focus and direction.

However you decide to go, establish a base from which to begin. Gather your power objects—crystals, essential oils, incense, drum, rattle—around you. Include your journal and maybe some crayons. Dress comfortably for the journey. Wearing special scents or essences can empower your journey. You may want to begin by drumming, rattling or chanting. Having your power objects around you while you drum or rattle is a most effective trance-invoking technique! Listen to the Goddess calling your name. When you feel that you have sufficiently prepared the ritual space in a way that works best for you, take your first step, draw the first Amulet and begin the Spiral Journey.

1. *Gifts and Talents*. The Amulet you choose at the center of the spiral reflects your innate gifts and talents. These are unique to you, your source of joy and inspiration. Your gifts can become burdens if you do not fully realize or use them appropriately.

Journal questions: *What did you enjoy doing as a child? Were you encouraged or discouraged? Were you rewarded for special talents in school? Are you still involved with the same or related activities? Do you value and appreciate your unique talents? Are you doing what you like to do on a regular basis? Are there certain gifts or talents that you've eliminated from your life in pursuit of another career or goal? Do you feel a loss for having done so? If so, how can you incorporate them into your life again? Are there times when you feel that you're not doing what you want to do? Do your talents go unacknowledged? Do you shy away from sharing your special gifts? If so, why?*

2. *Childhood Wishes*. This Amulet represents the dreams of your childhood. Within each of us is the childhood of dreams that came true and those that never unfolded. This Amulet can also reflect your childhood wounds and family conflicts.

Journal questions: *Your Goddess Guide at the second gate holds your hand for a journey into the sacred landscape of your child Self. (From* here on I'll use "child" to refer to your child Self.) The Amulet you choose holds you, comforts you and offers you the gift of heartfelt communication with your child. Imagine your child sitting on your lap. Imagine holding her in love and trust. How old is she? What does she look like? What is she wearing? What does she say to you? What are her expressions? What does she want you to remember? What does she want most of all? Does your child have a "secret" to tell you? Who does she feel comfortable with? How does she play? Who are her friends? Put the pieces of the family picture in place. What was going on in the lives of your parents at the time of your birth? Your grandparents? Your siblings? Does your child feel "at home" with the family? What—and who—is your child afraid of?

You may want to experience this exercise with your child at different ages. A five-year-old will have a different story from a ten-year-old or a teen. How do the stories differ? Using a piece of paper (large enough to accommodate the size of your child), trace an outline of what your child's body would look like. Using symbols, letters and shapes, let your child tell her story, marking and drawing directly on the body outline. Relate the story and experiences to places in your child body. How does your Goddess Guide help you?

3. *Secrets.* The Amulet you choose here reflects your secrets, which may include issues of shame, the fuel of lowered self-esteem.

Journal questions: *Begin by writing your secret or secrets in your journal. Remember, secrets sap strength by binding and blocking energy in unhealthy ways. Telling your secrets, if only to yourself at first, helps break through the denial that blocks the healing path. How many secrets do you have? Where in your body do you hold your secrets? Are some secrets bigger, more powerful than others? What are their colors? How much space do they take up? Do you have a symbol that represents them? Do you have secrets about other people? Is your intention to protect them? Are there family secrets? Most secrets are probably about sexual issues and those involving a cultural taboo. Do you have sexual secrets? Have you ever been hurt as the result of revealing a secret about yourself? About someone else? Has someone ever sworn you to secrecy as a means of holding power over you?*

Find a safe place to tell your secrets so that you can release trapped energy. Be gentle with yourself while unraveling the secret knots. Let your Goddess Guide offer comfort in the territory of your secrets.

4. *Pleasures and Treasures.* The Amulet you choose here reflects the way you experience pleasure in the world. This Amulet speaks of the joyful treasures that you have uncovered or those not yet found. It can also represent disappointments and disillusionments.

Journal questions: *Let the image on this Amulet talk to you. What does the image bring up for you? Does it remind you of a pleasurable thought or feeling, or a treasured moment? Do you know the experience of ecstasy? How do you experience joy in your body? What does joy look like? What are your disappointments? Let your imagination speak for your heart. Going deeper, you may want to take a look at lies you were told, lies you told yourself. Were there betrayals? Veils? Things you couldn't see because of distractions or coverups? In each of these areas, tell your story.*

In your journal, your visual diary, draw scenes or incidents that have most impressed your adult life. Who was there? Who was absent? What were your feelings, the senses in your body? What colors best describe your feelings? Take time to remember the pleasures and treasures of your life.

5. *Anger, Fear and Sadness.* Allow the image on this Amulet to reveal connections, feelings, situations, and experiences that involve anger, fear or sadness. All feelings are expressions of moving energy and have the power to heal. This Amulet also represents renewal.

Journal questions: *Can you be with your feelings? Can you be with your life? What does your _____ look like? Where do you hold your _____ in your body? What colors are associated with your _____? How does your body let you know you are angry, fearful or sad? Are there lingering resentments, little angers that keep popping back up, that you carry around with you? What triggers your _____? Who would not want you to experience anger, fear, sadness? What are your beliefs about these feelings? Do anger, fear, and sadness block feelings of joy, pleasure and ecstasy? In the center of your body, what takes up the most room?*

What are your most powerful memories and experiences associated with anger, fear, sadness? Who was present at the time? What were the details? How was the situation created? How did you respond or react? What did you feel or what did you want to say? What did you need in that situation in order to feel more comfortable? Do you need anything now for healing, releasing, transforming or taking care of your anger, fear or sadness? Is there anything you need now for revealing, renewing or enhancing your joy, ecstasy and pleasure? Use crayons to illustrate your experience. What Amulet did you pick? How does your Guide help you?

6. **Body, Mind, and Spirit.** Allow the image on this Amulet to reveal ways you experience the relationship among your body, mind, and spirit.

Journal questions. (Note: The word "body" is used in all these questions. Substitute "mind" and "spirit" for a second and third round of questions.) *How do you feel in your body at this very moment? Describe your body. Are there any areas where you are holding tension? What areas feel particularly relaxed? Are there areas of your body that you are uncomfortable with, that you have strong feelings for or against? Is there a part of your body that you think is dirty or offensive? What are your beliefs about this part of your body? What messages do you send it? How long have you felt this way? How can you integrate a healthier attitude of acceptance?*

What were your experiences of your body as a child? How were you held, touched and played with? How were you bathed, clothed and nurtured? How was affection expressed? How does your body "remember" these experiences? How were you disciplined? Did you experience verbal, physical or sexual abuse? Does your body "remember" these experiences? What are the consequences for you today? Did you experience childhood illness or diseases? Any accidents as a child? What were the details? Does your body "remember" the accident or illness? Do you experience physical or emotional consequences as an adult? Do you harbor any shame or blame related to the experience?

How does your mother feel about her body? How does she talk about or relate to your body? How does your father feel about his body? How does he talk about or relate to your body? If you have siblings, how do they relate to their bodies? How do you take care of your body? What is your experience with food? Exercise? Aging? Your sexuality?

Use these questions and issues to help foster an understanding of your relationship with your body. They are not meant to be answered like a physician's health report. Use them to trigger images and senses. Let your body, mind, imagination and emotions reveal your story.

Write about your experiences. Ask your friend to help you trace the outline of your body on a large sheet of paper. Indicate with color where your mind and spirit reside. Write stories or feelings about each aspect of your body around and inside the body tracing. Use crayons to draw symbols that relate to your experiences. This body "map" will give you a visual reference for your journey into the sacred story of your body. Be detailed and specific. The more you can remember, the more fully you come to know yourself. The more you awaken to yourself, the more you are able to fully live your own life.

The six steps spiraling outward involve essential personal issues. They are the foundation for building your present and future self. The pieces are woven together in a tapestry that reaches deeper and further than the sum of its parts. Working on issues of the past and taking care of yourself in the present can create an empowered, healing and fulfilling future. Knowing and remembering who you have been and who you are open the gate for union with your divine Self.

7. *Future Self.* Let this Amulet reveal the heart and voice of your Goddess self, fully integrated with the world around you. The Goddess Guide you receive here will accompany you in the realm of future visioning, helping you breathe life into the whole and healthy person you are meant to be. This Amulet is a guardian for planting, blossoming and fulfilling your dynamic and creative self, unencumbered, unburdened and wholly free.

Journal questions: *Write about your future. Let your mind wander. Imagine fulfilling a childhood wish. Imagine being free of old wounds. Envision your Goddess Self dancing and singing. Imagine loving ways to care for your body, mind, emotions and spirit. Imagine being filled with courage and strength for getting through challenging issues. How would that feel? Imagine short-, medium- and long-range goals that put your spiritual and emotional needs first, and how it would feel to achieve them.*

Visualize what you want yourself to be. Imagine talking to your Self in a voice that encourages, accepts and forgives. Imagine speaking a language of loving kindness, peace and understanding. Imagine breaking free of any limitations. Imagine laughing right out loud. Imagine following your heart's desire. Imagine fulfilling your divine purpose, sharing your unique gifts with the world.

Imagine finding forgotten, fragmented, broken and buried parts of your Self, lovingly nursing them back to life, weaving them into a radiant cape of Hope and Healing. Imagine living wholly connected with all of life's magical moments, belonging to your Self, creating your life the way you want it.

Remember that you are always — and in all ways — changing. Each time you take the Spiral Journey you will experience new Guides for each step, revealing unexpected and surprising pieces of your puzzle. You will come to new spiritual places for unlocking deeper dimensions of your Self. Map your journey. Mark your steps. Walk the Goddess Way. What you focus on will grow; focus on growing your Self. Meditate on each step, reflecting and honoring the sacred Wise Woman within.

The wisdom of each Amulet carries an ancient memory for honoring your Goddess beginnings, your natural and wild Selves. Your Great Goddess guides on the Spiral Journey will respond to you in very personal ways. The Spiral Journey is a journey of everyday magical life, transforming and renewing your Self in vibrant spiral time.

The Goddess Amulets

The Dreaming Goddess — Intuitive Inspiration

On the island of Malta in the Mediterranean are found several Goddess temples and tombs; they are approximately 6,000 years old — older than Stonehenge. Their location places them at the center of Neolithic Goddess culture. These sites are thought to have been healing centers in Neolithic times. The temples contained altars, alcoves, Goddess sculptures, pottery and figurines. Walls were carved with spiral designs and painted with red ochre. Pilgrims could spiral into the underground temples, listening to the echoes of the priestess providing healing nourishment as she channeled oracular visions from the Goddess. The Dreaming Goddess was one of the sculptures found in an alcove of an underground temple.

There is no evidence of weapons or warfare. This place may have been a sacred mystery "school" where priestesses of the Goddess came to learn and practice their healing arts, and a sanctuary for those seeking guidance from the Goddess and Her shamanic priestesses.

The Dreaming Goddess is a trance-channeling priestess who ventures deeply into the darkness for divine inspiration. She is an

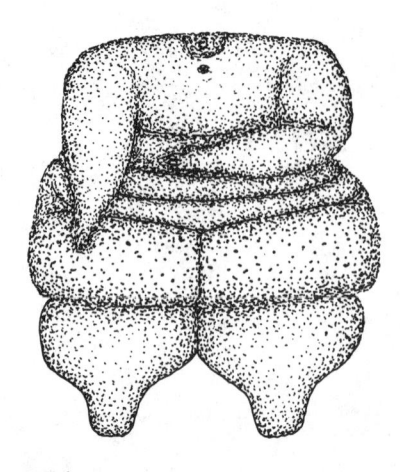

Mother Goddess or Priestess figure from Malta. Her contours are identical to many of the temple structures found on the island. This figure was uncovered with two other Goddess amulets in an egg-shaped subterranean chamber, perhaps an inner alcove for connecting with source energy. (AB)

Interwoven carved spirals from a megalithic stone at the Tarxien temple on Malta. This labyrinthine dance is an invitation into the sacred mystery of the dream. Approximately 5,000 years old. (LM)

oracle, dreaming visions of wholeness for personal survival and the benefit of the community.

When you get the Dreaming Goddess, this is no time for action. She reminds you to seek counsel and creative inspiration from your dreams, including daydreams. This means it's time to unplug your active, conscious self and connect with what lies just beneath the surface of the obvious — your subconscious. Let the Dreaming Goddess help you gather visions of what you know in your heart but that you have forgotten or pushed aside.

She arrives just in time. You've probably exhausted your mind in search of the perfect answer. But the answer you're looking for cannot be deciphered through logic or reasoning. Trying to figure it out can lead to obsessive thinking and put you in a tailspin, eventually leading to confusion and feelings of emptiness and dis-empowerment. It's perfectly okay to feel confused. Confusion is an ally, indicating that your heart, mind, and body are playing tug of war. Relax. There are no wars — no need for warriors — in the Garden of the Goddess. Daydream. Record your dreams. If you have trouble remembering them, make a dream pillow. Fill it with mugwort for stimulating dream activity. Include charms, talismans, affirmations and offerings. Climb aboard the Dream Boat for a journey to Malta, Island of Whispers and Inspirations, where your direction will be sanctioned by the Goddess, in harmony with your heart's desire.

When you least expect it, an answer will appear. You may not be able to grasp its meaning in a conscious way. Symbols and metaphor are the languages of dreams. Let the dream unfold and reveal itself, offering you a surprising gift. Feel the harmony when head, heart, and hands are joined in a unified response. Enjoy the process. The land of dreams is a paradise where magic happens. Remember, every bend in the river eventually finds its way to the ocean.

> *Affirmation:* I trust the wisdom of my dreams. I am willing to listen to and act upon their inspiration, knowing I will be led in the direction of personal growth and fulfillment.
> *Colors:* Indigo, black, royal purple.
> *Fragrances:* Mimosa (fresh flowers), clary sage (essential oil), mugwort (fresh or dried leaves).
> *Creativity/Meditation:* Dream Story.

Place your crayons and journal beside your bed. Before going to sleep, hold the Dreaming Goddess Amulet in your hand or put it under your pillow. If mimosa flowers are available in your area, place a bouquet on your bedside table. Briefly inhale essence of clary sage (prolonged use can provoke headaches) or crumble a few fresh leaves of mugwort, inhaling the fragrance with long, slow breaths. Imagine your breath is indigo or royal purple and the color flows gently in rhythm with your breath. Ask a question or make a wish, seeking guidance from your Dream Self.

Before jumping out of bed in the morning, reach over and grab the first crayon you touch, drawing the feeling or the vibrational experience of your dream. Use shapes, marks and broad strokes. For instance, euphoria might look like a big open circle, anxiety might be expressed by short, tight marks compressed in a small space, and so on. Stay with the feeling in your body, avoiding intellectual analysis. When you're done, title your dream drawing. Let the words flow, even if they seem silly, don't make sense or are in a language you don't understand. Later on in the day, see if the question you asked the night before has any connection to your dream "story." You won't have to force an answer. It may not come for awhile. But surely it will.

I titled one of my dream stories "Viva Karuna." I don't know where the expression came from and I didn't understand its meaning, except I knew "viva" meant "life" or "long live..." The words were on the tip of my tongue when I woke up and I laughed at their curious sound. But I'd come to trust my dreams implicitly, and without hesitation wrote them down. Later on, I looked up "karuna" in Barbara Walker's *Woman's Encyclopedia of Myths and Secrets*, always my first line of investigation. The word "karuna" is a tantric term meaning "mother-love" and embraces all forms of love including touching, tenderness, compassion, sensual enjoyment and eroticism. I had gone to sleep the night before feeling indecisive regarding my choices for the next group of Goddess sculptures to reproduce for my company. After sitting with "Viva Karuna" for awhile, I realized in a flash of insight that the next group would be "The Mother and Child Series." And I immediately began sculpting them. Viva Karuna! Of course.

Gorgon Goddess — Transforming Anger, Reclaiming Power

The Gorgon represents the Crone aspect of the Triple Moon Goddess. She is the serpent Goddess of the Libyan Amazons, often called the dragon of the darkness, symbolizing raw female instinct. The Gorgon mask symbolizes ancient Goddess power. The Moon-worshipping priestesses of the African matriarchies wore similar masks, called *gorgoneions*, during their sacred rituals to invoke the Goddess and guard the secrets of the blood mysteries. The faces on the Gorgon masks were painted with red ochre and surrounded by serpents, representing a woman's healing "wise blood" and the regenerative qualities of the Dark Moon Goddess.[1]

According to Greek myth, Medusa was one of three beautiful Gorgon sisters, sea Goddesses Who lived at the boundaries of night and death. While Her sisters were immortal, Medusa was mortal—symbolic of Her association with the death aspect of the Trinity.[2] When Poseidon seduced Medusa in Athena's sanctuary, Athena was outraged with jealousy and turned Medusa and Her sisters into hags whose frightful stare could turn men to stone. Perseus was tricked into slaying Her and presenting Her head to Athena. Oases sprang up where Medusa's blood flowed into the African desert.

Athena denied being born of woman, and claimed to have sprung forth from her father Zeus's forehead. She wore Medusa's head on her breastplate as a symbol of power, affirming her alignment with the patriarchy and its destruction of the matriarchal tribes.

Turning Medusa into a monster represents patriarchal efforts to separate the Death Goddess from the original Trinity. As

Greek Medusa with wings and double serpent belt. She wears the Gorgon mask, symbolic of her matriarchal origins and connections to the mysteries of the Dark Moon. Approximately 2,600 years old. Temple of Artemis, Corfu. (LM)

Hecate Triformis, Crone of the Night Roads. She holds the symbols that imbue her with primal power and immortality: a lighted lunar torch to guide the initiate's journey through the darkness, the key that opens the gate to birth, death, and regeneration, and a scepter that cuts through illusion. She was called "Queen of the Witches" and when angry was able to make all life stand still. From an engraved gem, Rome. (LM)

Greek invaders vanquished Goddess cultures, the Gorgon, like many other female deities, were relegated to darkness by a worldview that declared women inferior and menstruation "unclean," a taboo demonstrating patriarchy's fear of women's psycho-sexual power which is influenced by phases of the Moon and heightened during menstruation.

The Gorgon mask, once a symbol of women's power and identification with the Goddess, now represents the "horror, fear, and rage" that froze on the faces of the warrior women who were forcibly violated during one of the most devastating transitions of human social development.[3]

When you get the Gorgon Amulet, step back. She wants you to take a look at how you dance with anger. Angry, you may feel like the Dark Goddess Who has been banished from the realm of the living, not knowing what to do or where to go with it, not having an appropriate outlet to express it. Anger and anything "untamable," especially women's feelings, have been relegated like the Dark Goddess to the Underworld. Consequently, after feelings are repressed and separated from our conscious ability to use their enormous transformative energy, we become disempowered when they do surface. Anger usually rears its "ugly" head at inappropriate times, with a tremendous force that doesn't match the situation, and ends up getting stifled and inadvertently pressed into choking tears. If anger is repressed for too long, debilitating depression and self-destructive and addictive behavior often result.

Are you masking your anger, rage, or frustration, denying your instinctual, gut feelings? Do you feel "frozen" in an unidentifiable emotional state? Do you feel as if your rights have been violated in some way? Denying feelings blocks the healing power of the Gorgon, Whose wisdom weaves the mystery of rebirth back into life. Her mask no longer embodies the transformative qualities of the Moon, but becomes a rigid defense, blocking self-knowledge, sexual pleasure, and personal empowerment.

The Gorgon Goddess wants you to reclaim your power. Use your anger to gain greater self-clarity for reshaping your life. Discover new ways to create changes from old, imprisoning patterns. There's a spate of advice about what to do with your anger when you feel it. The first step is to know how it feels, getting in touch with how anger first "appears" in your body.

Intellectual analysis is not called for here. Let the body's wisdom lead the way. Stifling it, denying it, or distracting from it blocks the flow. My heart pounds, my face reddens, and my stomach tightens the very moment a situation triggers anger. Instead of reacting by "venting," or distracting myself from my feelings with analytical interpretations, I immediately bring my attention to my body, breathing into my angry places. By being fully present in my body I'm able to take care of me first; I flow with the energy as it enters and eventually works its way through my body. This practice also helps me break free from the old way I used to dance it.

In the past I was never able to communicate effectively while in "fight" mode. I would have duked it out, verbally or punitively, feeling worse afterwards, often getting physically sick. Now, once I'm fully aligned with my body, I manage my anger wisely, constructing, not destroying. Afterward, I tackle the challenge of effective communications, asking myself "What is the real issue here?" and "What do I really want to say?" Coming to courageous decisions, writing letters, making phone calls or directly confronting issues is often the last step.

The serpents on the Gorgon mask symbolize what Vicki Noble calls "snake power" or kundalini energy. The powerful transformative energy of the Goddess lies "coiled" at the base of the spine, waiting to be tapped to reveal insight, healing wisdom and divine prophecy for the benefit of the community. Vicki Noble says that yoga was most likely invented by menstruating women who learned to "master" the tremendous forces of the menstrual cycle.[4] If you have raised your "snake power," you are facing major transitions. The message of the Gorgon Amulet is one of deep psychic transformation, healing old wounds in the process.

Kali, Crone and Goddess of Darkness, is the primal female force of the universe. It is said that when Kali emerged, she filled the cosmos with a roar. She destroys in order to create anew. 19th century copper, southern India. (LM)

If your rage is overwhelming, seek guidance, particularly if it revolves around sexual abuse. Those who do not confront their incest or sexual abuse secrets and get counseling are very likely to suffer from alcoholism, drug abuse or depression. It's time to integrate the power of the Dark Goddess into the world of the living, restoring wholeness to the original Trinity. The Dark Goddess is the Crone—shaman and healer.

If you're resisting something, loosen your grip. Things wound too tightly break easily. Take a deep breath. Do yoga. Take a walk in nature. Hug a tree. Once confronted and understood, the Dark Goddess frees the initiate of fear, making way for rebirth and new growth—the Dark Goddess returning as the comforting Mother in the endless round of birth, death, and rebirth.

Let the Great Mother hold you in Her compassionate arms. Find your way back to the Goddess. Anger transformed can heal the world.

Affirmation: My angry feelings no longer scare me. I find appropriate places to share them.
Colors: Red and purple. Red fortifies passion. Purple promotes concentration, spiritual and intuitive faculties.
Fragrance: Ylang ylang (essential oil).
Creativity/Meditation: Angry Doll.

Channeling anger in creative ways is powerful medicine. Shamanic artmaking helps transform the invisible realm of feelings, ideas and visions into tangible images for promoting wholeness and harmony. The process that manifests imaginative spirit is a healing ritual often evoking euphoria. When I am in the creative "flow" I feel wholly connected to a vast and wondrous freedom, without limitations. I experience pure, sweet ecstasy, beyond time and space.

 Angry dolls give form to feelings. Images are powerful sources for healing. Gather whatever ma-

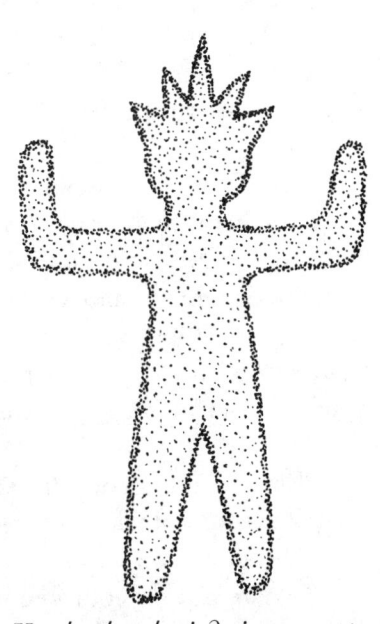

Use the above basic design as a pattern for your Angry Doll, cutting two identical pieces of cloth. Change the doll pattern in any way you like. Decorate with beads, embroidery, paint, yarn and any other materials you are drawn to work with. Before sewing it up, you may want to write an affirmation and place it inside. (LM)

terials you are intuitively drawn to; old clothes or new fabric, buttons, beads, yarn, markers, sticks, "stuffing" and embroidery thread are a good start. Establish your ritual space. Light a candle. You may want to play your favorite drumming music or ritual song. Rub a small amount of ylang ylang oil into your hands. Place the Gorgon Amulet before you. Focus on Her image, and the dynamic energy of Her expression. Invoke Her presence for guidance through the process of transforming your anger.

Cut out the shape of your doll, making the overall outline a bit bigger than you want the finished size to be. Work as large as you want. Make sure you have one piece for the front and one for the back. It's easier to do needlework on the separate pieces, having easy access to the underside for tying knots and stitching through. But sometimes I don't get "warmed up" until the doll is assembled. When she's sewn together, her angry expressions seem to come forth, having a form to fill.

Provide all the detail you can. Each portion of your doll's expression will animate energy. For inspiration, you may want to look at some Gorgon Goddess images. When completed, anoint your doll with ylang ylang oil. Bless yourself. Give thanks to the spirit of your anger for helping you feel your humanness.

> Bless you for your anger.
> It's a sign of rising energy.
> Direct not on your family.
> Waste not on your enemy.
>
> If you turn it into love,
> It'll bring you happiness.
> Bless you for your anger.
> It's a sign of rising energy.
> —Yoko Ono[5]

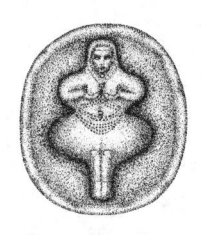

Inanna, Awesome Queen — Self-transformation

Ancient Sumerians called Her Awesome Queen of Heaven and Earth. Myths, hymns and poems in Her honor were repeated for hundreds of years, making Her the most celebrated deity ever to grace human imagination. The story "The Descent of Inanna" consists of more than 400 lines and was inscribed on clay tablets in cuneiform writing approximately 4,000 years ago.[6] However, Her story may have been repeated some 1,500 years earlier in the oral teaching tradition. Her poetic myth was told and enacted again and again as a means of absorbing the people into the regenerative cycles of nature.

Inanna's story invokes Her triple aspect as a Moon Goddess. As a young maiden, She is courted by Her paramour Dumuzi. As a mature, "flowering" and generous woman, She knows and shares the profound pleasures of Her sexuality. And as a wise and mature Crone, She learns the mysteries of death from Her journey into the Underworld, where She

Inanna, Queen of the Great Above and the Great Below, holds a date cluster in Her hand, life springing forth from Her shoulders and head. All are symbols of the power from within that nourishes and sustains new growth, whether psychic or in Nature. Vase fragment, Mesopotamia. Approximately 4,500 years old. (LM)

Mother Goddess Demeter and Persephone, daughter of renewal, are united in Spring. Each holds a flower, sign of Nature's cyclic return and a call to life. Marble relief from Eleusis, approximately 2,500 years old. Below, Kuan Yin, the Chinese Goddess of compassion and mercy. In Her quiet and soothing meditation, Her hands create a circle of serenity reminding us that peace resides within. Allow Kuan Yin to guide your journey with compassion. (LM)

passes through seven gates. At each one She is stripped of Her worldly adornments, and is eventually led naked to face Her sister, Ereshkigal, Goddess of Death; Her corpse is hung on a peg for three days.[7] After crying non-judgmentally for Her "dark sister," Inanna eventually returns as the awesome Queen of Heaven. She is then revived by two creatures made from the dirt beneath Her father's fingernails who bring Her food and water. When She returns, She must find a substitute to take Her place in the Underworld. Dumuzi and his sister Gestinanna share this task, each descending to the Underworld for half a year. This tale, similar to that of Demeter and Her daughter Persephone, is likened to the menstrual cycle and a woman's journey through powerful physical, emotional, spiritual and psychic transformation, eventually "returning" renewed.

Called by many names, Inanna was Goddess of plants, animals and the fecundity of all nature. She may be seen as all three female characters in the epic tale: Queen of Heaven, Queen of the Underworld and Sister (mother, lover and sister), representing the Trinity of Goddesses. In the patriarchal version, Inanna represents the Sun Goddess who "penetrates" the depths of Earth to bring forth new life.

Sylvia Perera relates Inanna's journey to the psychic and transformational journey of all women who "seasonally" venture into the unknown depths of despair, anguish and grief for retrieving the "lost feminine."[8]

When you receive the Goddess Inanna, She signals a time of awakening and activating your inner powers that shape your destiny and bring you closer to your "heart's desire." In the myth of Inanna, "From the Great Above Inanna opened her ear to the Great Below."[9] This tells us that Inanna *heard* something that prompted Her descent, inevitably bringing Her face to face with core issues. Often, the call to address hidden issues comes unexpectedly. I frequently tell my students that the voice of the underworld says, "Don't call us, we'll call you." The process is initiated by self-questioning or soul searching. Begin by asking a lot of questions. You may already be questioning the direction of your sacred path and the "powers" that have guided you thus far, or your motivation in a particular career or relationship issue. What has sufficed at one time may no longer be useful.

Questions are like lighthouses along the shore, guiding your journey home in foggy, stormy weather. One question is sure to shine the light on another, evoking yet another. Each question reveals and inspires personal truths that help you live fully attuned to your inner Self.

Inanna suggests you step into the heart of your child Self. With curiosity, wonder and spontaneity, ask yourself childlike questions: "What would happen if...?" "How would I...if I were going to...?" "When would such and such happen if I...?" Pay close attention to the questions; live and love them. Remember, most young children are not concerned with answers. Let your questions stimulate essential core energy. The answers will reveal themselves in time. Listen carefully.

The Goddess Inanna Amulet may also initiate a period of "mourning." This doesn't mean an actual death, but sorrow related to the grieving process. Inanna was released from the Underworld because She wept for Her sister Ereshkigal. Inanna wants to know if Sister Sadness is sitting at your core. If so, listen carefully to her message. Grieve whatever losses she may share with you. Cry for her—and with her. Express your sadness. Getting in touch with old and sometimes painful feelings heals old wounds and makes room for harmony, compassion, and serenity in your heart. The word "mourn" means "remember."

Affirmation: I have the courage to live my life closely attuned to my inner Self, my true nature. I cannot be something I'm not.
Colors: Golden yellow, indigo.
Fragrance: Rosemary (essential oil).
Ritual: The Spiral Journey.

When you receive the Goddess Inanna, She is calling you into the Spiral Journey (see p. 54), bringing you closer to your core, helping you get clear about issues that are coming up. It's not necessary to begin at the beginning. Let your intuition guide you. Projecting your logical mind onto the process may interfere with deep meaning waiting to awaken. Let the nourishing wisdom of the Goddess guide you from the heart to your future self.

Prepare your ritual space as suggested in the Spiral Journey. Wear something golden yellow, perhaps a scarf wrapped around your waist or flowing off your shoulders. Lapis lazuli is the stone often associated with Inanna. On Her journey, She wore a torc, a "power" necklace of small lapis beads. If you have some jewelry with lapis in it, wear it or your favorite ritual adornments. Light three candles to illuminate the triple powers inherent in Inanna. Anoint the Inanna Amulet with rosemary oil. Let yourself be drawn to a particular step and begin the Spiral Journey with Inanna as your guide.

The Laussel Goddess — Moon Time

This Paleolithic Moon Goddess was carved at the entrance to a sacred cave in the Dordogne Valley in France. She is called the Laussel Goddess and is approximately 25,000 years old. The original is nearly twenty inches in height and is sandy tan, painted with red ochre. She holds a crescent bison or ram's horn in Her right hand. Her left hand touches Her lower abdomen, gently resting on that place where the Moon resides within.

Essentially, She carries the first calendar in Her hand and in Her body. On Her crescent horn are carved thirteen marks which represent the thirteen full Moons and a woman's thirteen bleeding periods in a year: the rhythms of life in tune with movement across the sky.

Numerous early artifacts, including incised bone, stone and sticks, have been unearthed in and around caves. Alexander Marshack, using extensive microscopic research on the markings and "notations" carved in prehistoric artifacts, concludes that the marks are lunar calculations.[10] It was once believed that the marks were random and the artifacts belonged to male priests who ruled the clan! We now understand that these are the remnants of the first calendars that charted menstrual cycles and lactation and gestation periods, and were probably used by midwives.

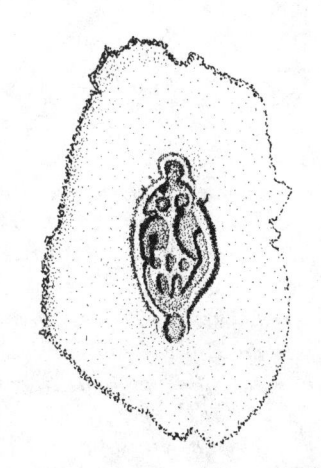

This carving from the interior of the Laussel cavern depicts a couple in lovemaking posture; it may have served in a teaching ritual involving the rhythms and cycles of menstruation, conception and gestation. (LM)

These early calendars were created to keep in touch with the harmony of life's forces that pulsed through the night sky and manifested in the rhythms of a woman's body. The effect provided a sense of unity. Life was not random or chaotic; it was connected with the natural and cosmic worlds, and its foundation was its relationship with the Female Source.

When you receive this Amulet, the Laussel Goddess is advising you to take your time and not rush around. If you feel compelled to justify your existence by what you do, you may be caught in a frenzy of never having enough time. Anne Wilson Schaef, in her book *Meditations for Women Who Do Too Much*, says that workaholism is the addiction of choice for those who feel unworthy. If the only time you get to rest is when you're completely exhausted, collapsing into a stupor, you need to look at your behavior and the issues that keep you constantly on the go. Unhealthy, habitual work patterns must end.

Are there feelings you are trying to avoid? Listen to your body. Your neck, back, shoulders or stomach may be telling you something. You may be taking on too much, feeling psychically overwhelmed. During certain times of the month, you may be very sensitive, picking up unwanted vibes.

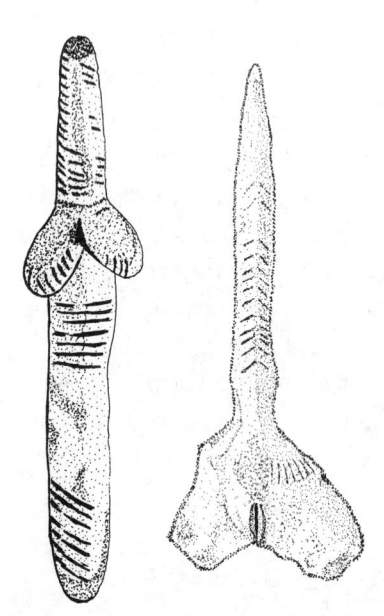

Left, carved breast "calendar" on bone charts menstruation, gestation and perhaps lactation cycles, marking the rhythms of a woman's Moon Time blood as early as 30,000 years ago. Dolni Vestonice, Czechoslovakia. Right, vulva "baton" with engraved sequential notations. Microscopic analysis shows the calculations were made with different tools at different times. Incised vulva clearly makes an association with female/lunar processes and may be a menstrual/pregnancy calendar. Approximately 17,000 years old. France. (LM)

Make an effort to become more aware of your Moon Cycle, recording ovulation, menstrual and post-menstrual times. If you're trying to conceive, listen to the rhythm of your cycle. Your body is a miraculous, dynamic being and knows how to take care of you, when you let it. Make sure you're not harboring sentiments that equate menstruation with "uncleanliness." Your attitude about your bleeding time can affect how you experience it in your body.

Take a recess. The Laussel Goddess invites you into Her delicious cave for a period of rest, relaxation and sensual solitude. Access the shamanic healing aspects of your menstrual cycle. Create a Moon Cave in your room. Arrange three or four oversized pillows in a "nest" on the floor. Drape them with red cloth. Hang red curtains from the ceiling, creating an enclosed area around the pillows. Decorate your Moon Cave with images that reclaim the power and mystery of your bleeding time. Spend quiet time writing, chanting, meditating. Listen to the voice of your Wise and Wild Woman within. Let her speak to you in visions and dreams. Invite other bleeding women into your Moon Cave.

If you are pregnant, create a Mother Cave. Spend time connecting with your child-to-be. Make your Mother Cave large enough to invite others to share with you this intimate time when your Moon blood is creating new life.

A Crone Cave can be made the same way. Decorate with empowering images of your Crone years. Establish an altar and make offerings to the Moon Goddesses,

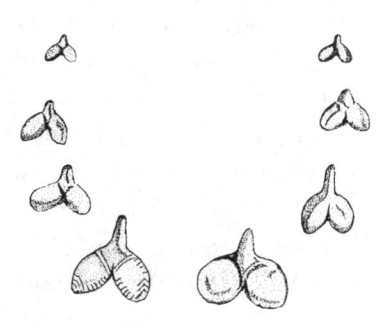

Notched double breast amulets strung together in a pendant. Several similar breast amulet pendants were found in Palestine, France, Switzerland, the Aegean, and Italy. They indicate highly complex methods of lunar observation and notation. This "power" pendant may have been worn by a shaman-midwife in a ritual-like teaching ceremony. Approximately 28,000 years old. Dolni Vestonice, Czechoslovakia. (LM)

your muses, and your spirit guide and guardians.

Mother Moon signals a strong emotional state. You might be feeling frazzled and want to scream. Duck inside Her sacred cave and let out a full holler. Or maybe you really feel like crying. Whatever emotion seems on edge, expressing it will release tension. The Laussel Goddess may also indicate feelings of vulnerability or rejection. Get to the underlying source of what may be disturbing you. Troubling or uncomfortable emotions might trigger compulsive or reactionary behaviors. Most destructive behaviors and addictions are based on the inability to calm ourselves. The wisdom of the Laussel Goddess teaches renewal through inner peace.

Follow your bio-rhythms. How do they correspond with lunar phases and transits? (There are a number of lunar calendars that will help you chart the Moon's passage through the constellations.) The energy of the New, Waxing, Full and Waning Moon is subtle yet powerful. And sometimes not so subtle! Get to know how each phase is reflected in your own cycle.

Moon time includes silliness. Originally, the word "silly" meant "blessed," as in Selene the Moon Goddess, who pulls the Moon across the sky in Her chariot. So let the Moon Muses tickle you pink. Humor heals.

Trust that while you're away, the world will not fall apart. When you return you'll feel renewed and refreshed. Moon time is sacred. Honor it and enjoy.

> *Affirmation:* I have time enough, courage enough, and love enough to take care of myself. I listen to the wisdom of my body and my own Moon cycles.
> *Colors:* Silver, crimson.
> *Fragrances:* Sandalwood (essential oil), camomille (tea).
> *Ritual/Meditation:* Moon Time Body Blessing.
> Keep track of your menstrual cycle; listen to your womb. Give yourself an "M" day, awakening to the lunar power of your blood cycle. Use the phrase "I'm in my power time" when talking about your sacred lunar bleeding time. Choose another Goddess Amu-

let to help guide you with a vision during this intensely psychic time. Drink herbal teas (no caffeine!), listen to relaxing music and read poetry. Write letters, write in your journal, take a bath or take naps. Carry the Laussel Goddess Amulet with you and imagine. . .

I am stunned and awestruck as I touch Her sacred stone carving. Her presence shakes me deeply. I feel this in my body, in my sense of being. I am experiencing Her within my body's breath. I am breathing and I know Her body as my own. I am breathing Divine Goddess breath, I am caressing myself with care and I am touching my body, over and over again with gentle feeling. I whisper my mantra of self-love over and over again. I am loving my wondrous and changing woman body, my Goddess body. I am a sacred living being.

I am counting the notches in Her Moon Horn, over and over. Thirteen is a sacred number, the letter M. She is Moon, Magic, Magnificent, Matter, Mother. She is Me. I am counting, marking signs and symbols of movement of the ever-changing crescent in the dark sky. I am marking time in my body and knowing Her body. And She is here with me. She is Divine Female, Great Mother, expressing the passage of time in bodies, my water body, changing light body, sky body.

I am here at the beginning where all life begins, is nourished, takes hold. She is my witness, my Guide and Divine Inspiration for sacred dancing and ecstatic trance, rituals for honoring the mysteries of Moon Magic flowing through all of life, through me time and time again.

The Great and Dark Earth nourishes me, nourishes the wise green plant foods as the infinite blackness of the night sky nourishes the birth of the Moon, Stars, Sun and the mysterious dark warm Womb. Mama, Mana, Mami is now giving birth, nourishing all my clan, my kin, my people, and I see Her creatures birthing anew in seasonal time.

I am painting Her carved stone body with red ochre clay, empowering Her form with the magical and abundant living blood of the Earth. And I am painting my own body blood red, deep red, running red. All of life pulsing, living red.

I am dancing and I am slapping the rhythm of time on my chest, on my thighs, on my belly, pounding the patterns of possibilities with my feet on the ground. I am howling Her songs, slipping into my mystery, spiraling dance in timelessness. In Her body She gathers abundance for bringing forth life and I gather the mystery of Earth, Air, Fire, and Water within me. She generates and nourishes bodies from Her own and I generate and nourish my sacred self.

Again and again She guides me and reminds me of body knowing, body healing, body changing wisdom. Over and over again she says, "Take care of your body, Wise Woman, Wise Woman." She is Divine Conduit, "can do it." She is a messenger from Moon Body to Woman Body to Earth Body and back again. She stands uniting all as one. And I am blessed in this oneness.

The Nile River Goddess —
Strength, Triumph, Success

The flooding of the Nile River was a beneficent gift bestowed by Divine Nature. The river's nourishing waters provided fertile soil and a complex and diverse ecosystem that included an abundance of plant and animal life along its shore. All life was birthed and provided for, decayed and regenerated in an endless round of Source and re-Source.

Birds and snakes marked seasonal changes in their migratory, nesting and birthing patterns, each sacred creature an epiphany of the Goddess of Life heralding a new season of cyclical transformation.

The religion of the Goddess in pre-dynastic Lower Egypt centered around the Cobra Goddess. An oracular sanctuary stood in the Egyptian city of Per Uto, dedicated to the Cobra Goddess, Ua Zit. Images of Isis and other animal deities show the Cobra "seated" on the forehead as if rising out of the third eye.

The symbol of the cobra was used to represent the Goddess in hieroglyphics very early on.[11]

This bird- or serpent-headed Goddess is from pre-dynastic Egypt and the original is approximately 5,000 years old. The hieroglyph *Ka* takes the same form as the gesture of the upraised arms and symbolizes an individual's mother soul who comes to join them in the afterlife: "Behold I am behind thee, I am thy temple, thy mother, forever and forever."[12] Many sculptures similar in gesture come from this period. The lower portion of the serpent-headed Goddess tapers to a rounded point; perhaps She was inserted into the ground in rituals and ceremonies. In all the sculptures, She raises Her arms to the cycling forces of the cosmos, drawing down dynamic lunar energy, celebrating powers of transformation.

Goddess cultures of pre-dynastic Egypt have been largely ignored as archeologists raced to the period of the "brilliant" pharaohs. Excavated unmethodically, the earliest sites have been overlooked and relegated to the "primitive" heap that constitutes prehistory in the eyes of patriarchy: limiting possibilities by limiting premises. However, one early text was preserved that claims the Goddess existed before anything else had been created.

The Nile River Goddess comes to you today renewing your strength, helping you know the experience of triumph. It's time to honor

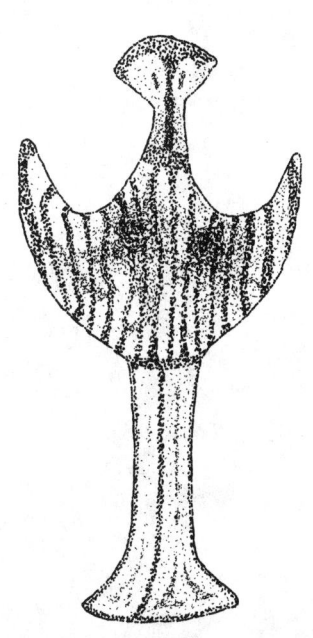

Bird-headed Goddess with Her wings/arms raised, greeting the divine forces of the Goddess immanent in all creation — the unseen numinous energy that informs all of life. The bird Goddess symbolizes female power centered in the heart. Approximately 2,300 years old, Tiryns. (LM)

The Goddess Amulets: The Nile River Goddess 🝊 *83*

where you have been, time to look at the "phases" that you have unfolded in your life, time to bless each moment from the place you started. Gather your life's harvest. Stand in triumph for all you have witnessed, sought for, lost and gained. Stand tall with your arms upraised in a gesture and exclamation of self-acceptance and certainty: "I am strong. I will go on."

Your Goddess Guide reminds you that you sometimes have to confront issues that you'd like to forget, deny or hope will go away. You may have to assert your own opinions. You may have to defy the written word to make your own valuable perspectives known, or face unwritten rules that have kept you stuck and stagnant. You can and will triumph, and each time you experience triumph, you create a memory in every cell of how good it feels, making the next time easier.

Like the river that flows with the cycles of the Moon, renewing life along the shore and carrying the souls of the dead back to the sea, you'll experience your own cycles of personal empowerment, stagnation and renewal of your strength through triumph. Remember that on the spiritual path, success can only be measured by the reflection of your heart.

Aphrodite, Mother of All Deities, is shown with Her crown of birds, Her ritual frame drum in Her hand. She was the ruler of time and fate, and governed Her peoples using Natural Law, the law of the Mother. In a gesture of openness and grace, She bestows Her blessing on you. Roman period. (LM)

Affirmation: I can and I will____.
Colors: Yellow, green, silver.
Fragrances: Nasturtium, freesia, lilac (fresh flowers), lemon (essential oil).

84 🍂 *Amulets of the Goddess*

Visualization/Meditation: Yes. Yes. Yes.

Stand before your altar or in front of your mirror and assume the posture of the Nile River Goddess. If possible, arrange a bouquet of freshly-cut flowers on your altar. Inhale the fragrance deeply. Repeat the suggested affirmation, filling in the blank. Imagine drawing sparkling silver energy down from the Moon, through your arms, flowing throughout your body. Feel the transformative forces of lunar vibrations pulsing through every organ, renewing and strengthening every cell. Practice this exercise each morning when you awaken and each evening before going to bed. Watch for visible manifestations of success.

> We daughters of daughters
> Rising Moon waters
> We wail and we wait
> And we listen
> We stretch and we soar
> Pushing for more
> We open our arms
> And embrace
> We sing out our songs
> Triumphing the storms
> We vibrate the night
> And rejoice

Ua Zit, Egyptian Cobra Goddess. She spoke the voice of the Goddess from Her oracular sanctuary on the Delta. 3,700 years old, Dessuk, Egypt, site of ancient Per Uto (Buto). (LM)

The Primal Mother Goddess and Child — Infinite Love

Serenely seated, Her child at Her breast, this Mother Goddess was originally a pottery vessel from the ancient Chimu culture of Peru. She symbolizes the fullness of the world, indeed, the fullness of the universe. Her "pot belly" is the container of life, created and nourished from a female Source. She is Pachamama, Peruvian Earth Mother, Goddess of Agriculture. In Peru, rituals are still performed in Her honor. Women travel long distances with offerings of thanks, sprinkling cornmeal on the fields, talking softly to the earth.[13]

This particular image resembles hundreds, even thousands of others from prehistoric cultures the world over. Their focus is the numinous and sacred act of creation. A mystery that all humanity shares is indicated by the smaller figure holding on to and being held by the Great Mother. In these images, the central fact is female, the overwhelming feeling unconditional love.

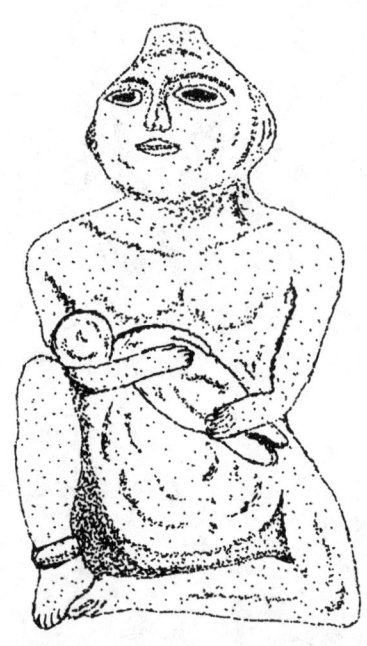

Northeast Woodlands Mother Goddess sits in regal splendor as She nurses Her infant in tenderness and grace. Imagine receiving unconditional love. Original is a clay vessel, symbolizing the transformative essence of female Source energy. Approximately 650 years old. (LM)

86 ❧ Amulets of the Goddess

The vessel as Mother Goddess is a fundamental concept in many traditional spiritual practices. The sacred earthen vessel is often presided over by priestesses. Among most primal peoples, women make pottery. Once made, a vessel's libations, ambrosias and unguents are administered by the wise women healers. Only in "advanced civilizations" does pottery-making become a man's occupation.[14]

When you receive the Mother Goddess and Child, it means you are ready to receive wholehearted and profound nurturing in body, mind, emotion and spirit. You've probably been very busy nurturing others. Now, at home or work, in meditation and ritual, counseling and prayer, with family and friends, you'll be surrendering to the majestic mystery of love. Until now you may have underestimated love's power, or limited love to certain definitions. Considering all you've been through in the name of love, it's perfectly understandable.

You are now in the embrace of an awakening power of love whose dimensions will take you beyond anything you've ever experienced. In your imagination you will see it; in your dreams you will feel it; in your heart you will know it: love that knows no limits, no conditions; love that listens without judgements or punishments. It is an experience of being held tightly

Seated Bird Goddess holds Her male infant in Her "wing" as She is showing off Her creation to the Universe with pride and admiration. Her body is a throne, the solid foundation of Earth. The Bird Goddess heralds the arrival of new life; Her creation is an epiphany, an appearance of the sacred. 2,550 years old, Boetia. (LM)

in the arms of a divine and Elemental Mother Goddess. She is infinitely One and All. She cares. And you are alive in Her bliss.

Affirmation: I am joyously alive with love. I feel inner peace and a sacred oneness with all life.
Colors: Earth reds, green, pink.
Fragrances: Rose (essential oil), lavender (essential oil), hyacinth (fresh flowers).
Visualization/Meditation: A New Vision of Love.

Drape a piece of red cloth across your altar space. Rearrange your altar images around it. You may want to anoint your cloth with a favorite fragrance. Try using the essence of rose or lavender. A fragrant bouquet of fresh flowers will intensify the experience. Light a red candle. With your Amulet in your left hand, hold it to your heart, the image facing you. Cover your left hand with your right. Breathe deeply into the center of your heart and belly. As you stand before your altar, repeat aloud the above affirmation. With your eyes gazing into the center of your candle, imagine iridescent pink and green vibrations gently soothing your "Goddess" heart, pulsing from your Amulet into your left hand around and through your heart center, gently flowing throughout your entire body, returning into your right hand and back to your heart again, soothing your "child" heart. Let the fiery energy of love intensify as you visualize first being the Mother Goddess in this Amulet and then the smaller "child" figure. Imagine feeling an

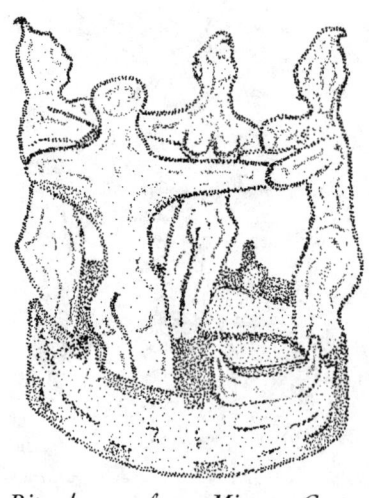

Ritual scene from Minoan Crete. Participants are joined in celebration of the delight and beauty of Nature and the Goddess Who is an integral part of their lives. Imagine dancing in the circle of infinite love. Approximately 4,300 years old. (LM)

infinite flow of love that weaves between you, the Goddess and you, Her child. Feel every cell awaken and tingle. Before you finish, ground the energy. Direct the vibrations of love down through your feet, into the heart of Earth for renewing love's life-giving energy.

When you've completed this meditation, cut off a piece of the scented cloth and carry it and the Primal Mother Goddess and Child Amulet with you for remembering that love of life, love of self, love of all beings is a powerful union that begins first in your own heart. Envision, nurture, and share a healthy and whole vision of love.

> How might your life have been different, if, deep
> within, you carried an image of the Great Mother,
> and, when things seemed very, very bad, you could
> imagine that you were sitting in the lap of the God-
> dess,
> held tightly . . .
> embraced, at last.
> And, that you could hear Her saying to you,
> "I love you . . .
> I love you and I *need* you to bring forth your self."
>
> And, if, in that image, you could see the Great
> Mother looking to Her daughters, looking to each
> woman to reveal, in her own life, the beauty,
> strength, and wisdom of the Mother.
>
> How might your life be different?[15]

The Dancing Bird Goddess — Ecstasy

In shamanic practices, ecstasy is the experience of wholeness and oneness with all, often accomplished by "flight" to the spirit world for communion with the forces of life, sexuality, and death. The shamanic state can be initiated by drumming, dancing, fever, menstruation, chanting, yoga, art meditation, fatigue, childbirth, psychoactive drugs and near-death experiences; it is often described as a merging of one's personal identity (ego) with the landscape, animals, deities, or ancestors.

Female healers were the first shamans and guardians of life, giving birth and acting as midwives. Vicki Noble makes the point that all shamans, no matter what their culture, always work in the realm of the feminine. They invoke the "Mother of the Animals," the "Mother of All Things," the "Dark Mother," "Grandmother Growth," or the "Death Goddess." Some form of the divine female realm is conjured to perform shamanic acts of healing.

Noble says the shaman "must in the long run" commune with the Goddess.[16]

In *Shamanic Voices*, Joan Halifax, whose extensive work as an anthropologist into Buddhism and shamanism has uncovered a wealth of information regarding these richly diverse traditions, weaves together "earth and sky." She says that shamans are the artists and poets; singers and musicians; dancers and writers. Shamans are also spiritual and politi-

Isis, known as the Source of Life, lifts Her protective wings to welcome the initiate into Her shamanic healing ecstasy. From a carving approximately 2,600 years old. (LM)

90 Amulets of the Goddess

cal leaders, storytellers and the keepers of cultural wisdom. They administer justice. Comedians, entertainers and actors, who help transform reality, are shamans. Counselors and psychologists work in the realm of the shamanic.[17]

Shamans have knowledge of the healing properties of plants and herbs, animal allies and Earth elements.[18] They are gatherers and foodmakers. They are sacred messengers who awaken feelings of awe and wonder, having developed an intimate relationship with the forces of creativity, sexuality, life, and death.[19]

The word "ecstasy" comes from *ek-stasis*: to be outside oneself. Ecstasy is a disconnection from daily, routine activities and patterned ego responses in order to receive information from a divine source. Female sexuality, in which orgasm can be so intense as to induce a state of ecstatic trance, figures prominently in ancient shamanic healing rites. *The Great Cosmic Mother* tells us that the "first religion" was originated by women and based on "sexual-spiritual" union: a celebration of body-based cosmic ecstasy.[20]

Today, a call to shamanism is often signaled by an accident, health crisis, or emotionally "hitting bottom." An initiate may travel uncharted psychological terrain when facing a near-death experience, receiving and remembering healing information in this extraordinary reality. During this time, those whose defenses are rigid and isolating are able to release resistance and let others in

This powerfully evocative Cretan snake Goddess portrays the natural grace and vital energy of the primal priestess/shaman who holds the powers of life, death and regeneration in her hands. Her animal ally, a bird, sits atop Her crown of roses. Approximately 3,600 years old, from the Palace of Knossos. (LM)

to help, opening the heart center to love and healing energy. Returning, the initiate often becomes a healer herself. I have heard many recovery stories from alcoholics, shamans in their own right, who "woke up," turned their lives around and became substance abuse counselors and therapists. Shamans are the "wounded healers" who speak from experience when they say "I know, I've been there."

The bird whose migratory patterns heralded the changing seasons and "foretold" the weather also laid the great Cosmic Egg of many a culture's creation myth. And the snake whose ability to shed its skin and return renewed from the belly of the Earth Mother evoked a powerful metaphoric symbol of the Regeneratrix. It seems apparent that bird- and snake-costumed shamans would hold particular power in the magical realm of "stirring" ecstatic experience. Because we live so disconnected from nature and the mystery and awe of the animal world, it's very difficult for us to grasp the impact of shamanic ritual, dance or celebration if we haven't experienced it ourselves, in our bodies.

The image on the Amulet is from a Minoan seal impression; the original is approximately 3,500 years old. Anthropomorphic bird- and serpent-headed deities and shaman figures have been found from the early Paleolithic through present-day traditional cultures. In the Neolithic Mediterranean regions which included matriarchal Crete, images of the Bird and Serpent Goddess abound. Images of Her priestesses show them hold-

Aphrodite, in what appears to be "shamanic flight," rides on the back of Her swan of good fortune. She carries a snake in Her right hand and a small "casket" in Her right, symbolizing Her knowledge of the mysteries of life and death. 2,600 years old, Boetia. (LM)

ing snakes, staring in trance. The snake, whose venom in very small doses produces a hallucinogenic, mind-altered state, may have played a significant role in the shamanic practices of these ancient cultures.

This particular image evokes a powerful vision of the serpent-headed Bird Goddess, a shaman woman with bare breasts and outstretched wings, dancing a sacred rhythm of ecstasy. Above her head is perhaps another snake whose rattle guides her journey to the spirit world. Or it may be the aura of a lightning flash of insight at that moment of divine and ecstatic communion with the Creatrix, Source of All Life.

When you get the Dancing Bird Goddess, She reminds you that your diligent soul-searching and arduous life bring a reward. Now you can dance the ecstasy of your own life into being. You are a fearless and courageous "technician of magic" who can transform reality, finding keys to unlock doors that once were closed. What you ask for, you receive. Information comes to you easily; the Snake Goddess is a messenger. The truth of the matter is in your hands and you know how to shape it. Use the energy to confront or challenge issues.

Shamanic experiences are not always fun. Your daily identity may be cracking and falling away, allowing your more authentic self to push to the surface. This may feel like you're "losing your head" or being torn apart. You may feel an inner fire in the form of hot flashes or bursts of insight as your energy is agitated, exciting change. A raised temperature or fever is a natural bodily response, triggering a call to healing action. Let the experience reveal wisdom and wholeness. Surrender to the transformation. The majestic Phoenix is born from the ashes of an all-consuming fire. What is changing in your life right now? What do you envision being born from this shamanic healing experience?

The Dancing Goddess is a sign that "magic is afoot." Your passion and sexual energy may feel unusually heightened. You might feel fiery, ready to embark on an intimate relationship.

Like the shaman, you're able to channel your energy in healthy, healing ways.

Contact your animal allies and spirit guides. Set aside the nine Sacred Animal Amulets and choose one. Her awesome power can amplify the magic already present. Go ahead and ask for what you want. Be prepared to receive what you ask for.

> *Affirmation:* The Goddess is alive. Magic is afoot. Goddess energy flows through me and I feel the ecstasy of my life.
> *Colors:* Red, indigo blue, black.
> *Fragrances:* Rosemary (essential oil), clove (dried, crushed buds), bay (essential oil, fresh or dried leaves).
> *Visualization/Meditation:* Shaman Dance.

Stand before your altar or a mirror. Play chanting or drumming music to ease into a trance state. Anoint your Amulet with one of the fragrances suggested above, or use one of your favorites. Breathe deeply, inhaling the aroma. Relax your shoulders. Each breath fills your body with vibrant red energy. You feel relaxed, your awareness expanding. Ask for something. Make a wish. Imagine that you spread your wings and soar with the Dancing Bird Goddess and your animal ally to the realm of spirit to retrieve what you want. Imagine finding it. Nestle it under your wings. Protect it. Bring it back with you. Stay open to the experience and whatever words, thoughts or images come up for you. When you "return," ground the energy by dancing your wish into being. Play your favorite music. Dance wildly, becoming one with your wish, your new reality. Dance until you can hold the ecstasy of your own life in your arms. To wind down, walk in a circle, clockwise three times. Make note of your experience in your journal.

> Woman like the big eagle am I,
> Woman like the opossum am I,
> Woman who examines am I,
> Woman like the hunting dog am I,
> Woman of justice am I,

Woman of transactions am I,
Woman like a clock am I,
Woman who stops the world am I,
Woman who divines am I,
Woman of the big star am I,
Woman drummer am I,
Woman serpent am I,
Woman like the wolf am I,
I show my power.[21]

Sheela-Na-Gig — Honoring Choices

This particular Sheela-Na-Gig carving forms one of the corbel supports of the church of St. Mary and St. David in Kilpeck, Herefordshire, England. Christian churches throughout Europe were built on temple sites (sometimes wellsprings and Earth energy lines) of the pagan communities that lived and practiced the "religion" of the Goddess. Many early Irish and English churches incorporated pagan images as a way of "accommodating" what couldn't be easily eliminated. By the 16th century, Church and State were consolidated in centralized power and forcefully abolished pagan customs.[22] In the

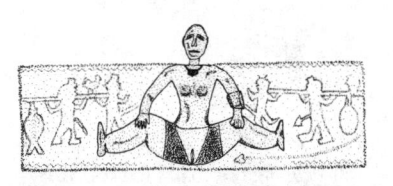

This wood carved Ancestor Spirit was placed above the entranceway to a men's ceremonial house. Unmarried men passed "between her legs" in a gesture of embodying the divine female spirit. In a ritual gesture of openness similar to the Sheela-Na-Gig, Her sacred yoni is celebrated and honored. Palau, Micronesia, early 20th century. (LM)

countryside, where pre-Christian practices were difficult to reach and suppress, the seasons, sexuality and celebrations of the Goddess continued.

In Celtic Britain, Sheela images were placed above church doorways. Most were removed from churches during the establishment of Christianity with its revulsion for anything "of the flesh," which usually meant female sexuality. Presently there are over seventy known Sheelas in Ireland and twenty-three in Great Britain.[23]

Naked and squatting, the Sheela-Na-Gig figure's bawdy gesture and enigmatic smile suggest that She knows the mysteries and origins of life, and surely which road to take to get there. Her image is similar to the yonic statues of Kali that still appear above the doorways on Hindu temples where visitors lick a finger and touch the yoni for good luck. Many of the carvings have deep holes worn in them from so much touching. According to Barbara Walker, the name Sheela-Na-Gig is probably derived from "yoni woman;" *gig* means female genitals; the French *gigue* is the name for an orgiastic dance in pagan times; a *gig* referred to the holy yoni in ancient Sumer, and the sacred temple harlots were known as *nu-gig*.[24]

The Sheela-Na-Gig may have served the same purpose in Irish pagan thealogy as the Baubo in ancient Greece: a ribald clown who danced her bawdy gestures at the Eleusinian Mysteries to restore joy and sacred sexuality

This Aboriginal rock painting visually depicts a creation from Western Arnhem Land in which All-Mother, the Snake Goddess, the old woman, gave birth to the ancestors. In many contemporary Aboriginal tribal myths, women elders sing teaching songs in ritual ceremonies that tell of a girl's first bleeding, clitoral pleasure and its importance in lovemaking, "sexual magic" and childbirth. (LM)

when Demeter grieved the loss of her daughter Persephone and the world was denied her power of fertility.[25]

In Japanese mythology, a Baubo figure named Ame-no-uzume-no-mikito, Alarming Female, performed a similar dance to draw Amaterasu, the Sun Goddess, out of Her cave where She was hiding, denying Her lifegiving light and radiant heat to the world after arguing with Her brother the Thunder God. The Baubo represented a shamanic healer who responded to the "alarm" and entertained the Great Mother long enough to restore life to the world. Barbara Walker reminds us that the well-being of the world needs female sexuality and enjoyment, relieving female sadness.[26]

Wherever She found Herself, She was acknowledged as a guardian along the pathway to communion with sacred life forces.

The nature of being, knowing and becoming is a profound consequence of making choices for yourself. If you have called upon the guidance of Sheela-Na-Gig, you are asked to honor your many choices regarding the issue at hand. Make a list. Carefully go over your choices. Get to know them. All choices are opportunites. Which choices are essential and appropriate to where you are now and where you want to go? Which choices address the questions you're asking? Which choices can be postponed or negotiated, and which cannot?

Choices are inevitable, and facing the many complexities of choice-making is not an easy task.

Isis rides a sow carrying a mystical ladder. In Her openness, She displays Her vulva with pride, suggesting that the numinous female principle is the gateway to the sacred. Hellenistic, Southern Italy. (LM)

The Goddess Amulets: Sheela-Na-Gig 🌀 97

Taking risks provokes anxiety. But the real risk is pushing through your anxiety and coming out with something new at the other end. Ultimately, the most important question to ask is: What choice is a reflection of my truth?

With wise and gentle laughter, Sheela-Na-Gig reminds you that the path of wholeness is always under construction. You are choosing and creating each step as you take it. Because the journey you are about to embark on may be unfamiliar, you have to gather your bricks, sticks, mud and stones, laying them in front of you each step of the way. As you re-construct your path you are also re-constructing the values that make up your choices, inventing your life as you go. Make healing choices that are Self-defining and Self-actuating, empowering your journey along the Goddess way.

One of the challenges in making choices is the ability to live with ambiguity just before your decision is made. Get to know the territory of ambiguity. Like a dog that walks around a spot several times before settling in, get to know where you're planning to go. When you make a choice that speaks from your heart, from blissful union with your Self, you'll

Clay Baubo figure from Asia Minor who like Sheela-Na-Gig displays her vulva as a ritual act of stirring the life force to promote transition. Approximately 2,400 years old. (LM)

marvel at the magic that follows. Honor your choices. They are your allies, challenging and enriching personal growth. Remember the healing energy of laughter as you stand before "the gate." Let Sheela-Na-Gig dance a smile on your face as you contemplate your next step.

Affirmation: I am reclaiming and reinventing my life. I can make mistakes, meander, and have fun along the way. The choices I make are all mine.
Colors: The rainbow.
Fragrance: Peppermint (essential oil).
Visualization/Meditation: Allying Ambiguity.

Sit comfortably. Anoint yourself with a drop of oil of Peppermint. Holding the Sheela-Na-Gig Amulet in your hand, take long, slow breaths and focus your attention on your breathing. Imagine that you are about to make an important decision with several choices, options and considerations. Before taking a step, rest in the place of "not knowing." Imagine a swirl of rainbow colors all around you. Explore possibilities. Familiarize yourself with the consequences of each choice. The spiritual traveler does not dive into an empty pool. How do you want it to feel emotionally in your body and mind when you take your first step? What is it like *not* to have an answer? How long can you sit with ambiguity? Make ambiguity your friend before you make a choice. When you're ready, imagine going through the doorway just below the place where the Sheela-Na-Gig sits. Touch her in passing for good luck!

Double Dutch jump-roping is a great adult exercise for learning how to get into the rhythm of ambiguity. I can still feel the sensation in my body of the front-to-back motion that preceded the perfect, decisive moment of jumping into the ropes.

This synchronized bodily movement is also what a tennis player uses, bobbing back and forth, waiting to return a serve.

Until it's "right" in your body, don't jump.

I am being and becoming in this moment of time.
The choices before me are truly mine.
Each one a seed in the darkness waits.
As I take my steps I face each gate.
I am listening deeply to the smile within.
A point of knowing will soon begin.
Healing choices speak their softness.
Whichever way I choose to go.
At any time, I know I'll know.

The Willendorf Goddess — *Belonging*

The Willendorf Goddess, originally carved in limestone and unearthed near Willendorf, Austria, is approximately 30,000 years old. She was found in 1908, nestled among tools, implements and crystals. She is the oldest sculpture of a human form yet uncovered. She represents the primordial Female Deity who gave birth to all of Creation out of Her bountiful body. She is a Divine Ancestress, embodying a pervasive female principle: parenting, sustaining and linking all peoples in totemic, cohesive unity.[27]

Hand-held, "portable" Goddess figures and amulets carved in stone and bone exaggerated Her round and "abundant" body, symbolizing the bulk and stability of Earth. Breasts, belly and buttocks swelled with possibilities. She was the One who gave birth to All.

Like the Earth, the Goddess possesses dynamic, creative energy that directs and holds life together. She is faceless, Her head bowed as if looking into her own body temple and what might be. Perhaps she looks into the Earth, realizing Her Source and the relatedness of all things. Her arms are resting across Her breasts. Does She offer nourishment for sustaining life? Does She offer the sense of belonging, of being "connected?"

Not meant as an individual portrait, She symbolizes the divine Creatrix whose mystery resonated deeply in the hearts, minds and magic of early peoples. The feet of most of these early Goddess sculptures are pointed, possibly to stick in the Earth — establishing a sense of place where cosmic forces could be generated, focused and grounded. A Divine Female presence was the core of religious, artistic, psycho-sexual, and ceremonial expression for possibly the first 200,000 years of human life!

You have called the Great Mother of Belonging to you for comfort, to remind you that your presence counts. You are connected to all existence by virtue of being alive, by being yourself. The feeling of belonging is an enormously powerful spiritual experience. It is also a socially, politically and personally expansive way of being in the world. If you are feeling discon-

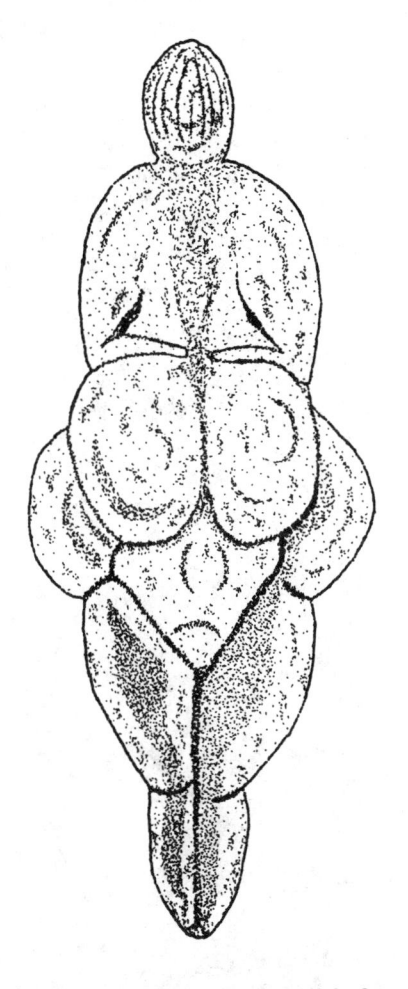

Lespugue Goddess. Her small, bird-like head and the repetition of egg shapes around Her body reveal an intimate connection with the natural world, creating and belonging to all that is. Ten vertical lines carved below Her buttocks on the reverse side indicate the ten lunar months of gestation. Approximately 25,000 years old, Paleolithic France. (LM)

nected or alienated, you are in a state of forgetting.

This Goddess Guide is always a call to return to Earth. Get your two feet back on the ground. Return to your own Source, your own resources. Get your eyes off "the other" (people, places and things). Bring your attention to focus on your own bounty, concentrating on where you belong, rather than on where you don't. Avoid distancing and devaluing habits such as comparing yourself with others, which always lead to feelings of isolation and loneliness. Take a few moments for deep breathing or meditation. Say "I love you" while looking into a mirror. Make a phone call to a friend and say "I love you." Give thanks.

Focused energy can be a powerfully moving and generating force. From a place of belonging wholly to yourself in love and acceptance, you will grow.

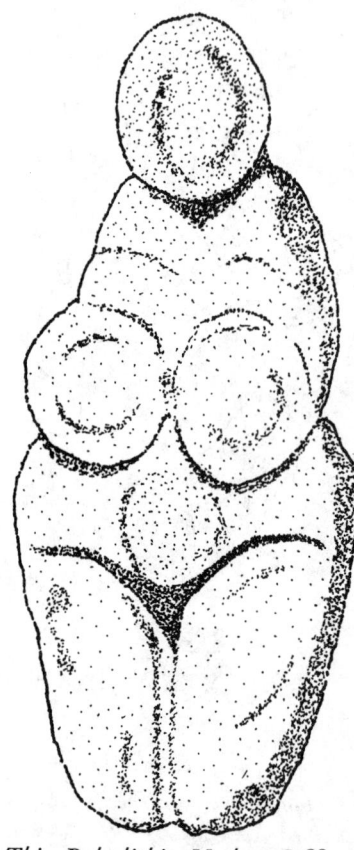

This Paleolithic Mother Goddess evokes the feeling of solid self-assurance as so many of the handheld, portable "Venuses" of this period do. Imagine looking into the center of your body and saying "I promise never to abandon myself." (LM)

Affirmation: I belong. A child of the Earth, I am guided and guarded by the Goddess. She holds me. She holds me. She holds me. And She will never let me go.
Colors: Brown, green, red, black.
Fragrances: Cedar (essential oil or incense), pine (essential oil), patchouli (essential oil).

102 Amulets of the Goddess

Visualization/Meditation: One Family.

Sit comfortably. Light a red or green candle. Anoint your Willendorf Goddess Amulet with one of the suggested oils, or use your favorite. Repeat the above affirmation inhaling the aroma deeply into your body. Imagine vibrant green energy flowing throughout your body with each breath. Relax. As you breathe, you release tension. With your next breath, imagine the vibrant green energy flowing outward, linking you with the generation that came before you: your parents, their siblings, cousins, friends and acquaintances. You don't have to know them all by name, but get a general feeling of their presence.

With the next breath, imagine the green vibrant energy joining your parent's generation with your grandparent's generation. Continue linking generations, letting the green ribbon of energy unite and bond you with your entire family.

In your journal, create an image that expresses your sense of belonging to one family.

The Sacred Animal Amulets

Cat — Protecting Good Fortune

Feline divinities were protective forces throughout ancient cultures. From the Paleolithic to the present day, the cat figures powerfully in our hearts and imaginations. An engraving of a lioness from a cave wall at Les Trois Frères in France (approximately 18,000 B.C.E.) portrays a sense of majestic, calm courage. Her form flows along an inner chamber alongside vibrant, colorful, sensitive and dramatic paintings. The cat's spirit, imbued with magic, came alive in the shadow dance of a cave fire, a living vision for communing with the pulse of the Great Mother. Each shamanic ritual served as a means of maintaining close contact with the mysterious and invisible forces of life, death and rebirth, for the enhancement and assurance of survival.

Leopards and lionesses acted as guardians during birthgiving and other initiatory rites. Strong, ferocious, secretive, playful, and regal, the feline is a powerful epiphany of the Mother Goddess. At Çatal Huyuk, one of the oldest and most important Neolithic Goddess sites in the Near East, the lioness appears to be the totem animal of this flourishing Neolithic Goddess culture. An awesome Mother Goddess seated on Her throne at the very moment of birth, the baby's head just visible between Her thighs, is flanked by two leopards. Their tails wind up Her back and wrap over Her shoulders, as if "grounding" cosmic energy into earthly life. On one of the site's shrine walls, two leopards stand face to face, modeled in plaster and richly decorated with red paint. They evoke a numinous, protective Goddess presence.

Sekmet and Bast are Egyptian cat deities. Sekmet, Goddess of fate, rules over the destiny of humanity. She is a solar Goddess, reigning with blazing fury. Bast is gentler, guarding Her "litter" with tenderness. Bast's festivities were celebrated by worshipers singing and feasting in ecstasy and pleasure. In one image, Bast is shown carrying the sistrum, symbol of lovemaking and joyous dancing.[1] The opposing qualities personified by Bast and Sekmet already indicate patriarchal fragmenting of the once-universal Goddess.

In a Khmer myth, Sinh, a highly revered temple cat, was the oracle of the Goddess Tsun-Kyankse, who ruled over the transmutation of souls. None could evade Tsun-Kyankse's piercing eyes of sapphire. Sinh, yellow like the amber body of the Goddess, saved the temple from invading forces by giving instructions in the form of an "imperious gaze" to close the temple doors, thwarting the enemy's advance.[2]

On Crete, images of the Goddess and Her lion companions

Two views of Birthing Goddess with feline protectors. The tails of each leopard wrap around Her shoulder, grounding and centering Her energy. Her child's head has just emerged. 8,000 years old, Çatal Huyuk. (LM)

106 ❧ *Amulets of the Goddess*

abound. In one image, the Goddess stands atop a womb-like mountain throne holding out Her sacred wand, the Tree of Life. Two guardian lions stand on either side of the mountain, affirming Her divine authority.

The Jaguar deities of pre-Columbian Central America are alive with the mystery of the spirit realm. Jaguar masks were used in sacred ritual, invoking feline powers: fierce and stealthy.

Nocturnal and associated with the Moon, cats are well known witches' familiars. Witches were regarded as shape-shifters who could turn themselves into cats nine times during their lives—no doubt relating to the Ninefold Goddess. The nickname "pussy" refers to both cat and yoni. The willow is sacred to the witch, and the appearance of cat-like tufts or pussy willows are the first signs of spring and the indication of forthcoming festivities. Because cats were considered the devil in disguise by Christian authorities, they were burned by the thousands along with witches during the Christian witch craze. The destruction of so many cats probably contributed to the increased rat population and ensuing plague.

The Cat Goddess on this Amulet is from the Native American Calusa culture in Florida. Found on a peat bog on Key Marco Island, She is approximately 1,100 years old. One of several exquisite ceremonial pieces carved from wood, She is the only artifact re-

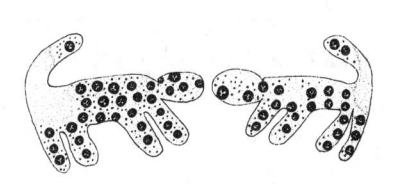

From the Leopard Shrine at Çatal Huyuk, these guardian felines are repeatedly decorated with plaster and earth pigments, revealing nearly forty layers of "paint." Whatever rituals were enacted, the bold and numinous presence of these deities was essential. (LM)

Fierce, protective and courageous, this lioness was carved on a wall from a site called the Chapel of the Lioness at Les Trois Frères in France. Approximately 16,000 years old. (AB)

The Sacred Animal Amulets: Cat 107

maining intact. She sits in regal splendor fixing Her fiery gaze upon all who pass.

The Cat Goddess is the bearer of good fortune Who also suggests you "guard" what you have gained. You have probably jumped through a few tight hoops to get where you are. You may have spent half your life putting out emotional "fires." Unconsciously, you may have started them to keep yourself busy, perpetuating a false and distorted sense of self-worth based on patriarchal perspectives that posit "taking care of others" as the ultimate self-sacrifice. You may have gotten "burned" along the way, feeling resentful or being resented. That behavior is all part of an old way of being. The Cat Goddess heralds the burst of new life. Giving *and* receiving are both spiritually rewarding. Prepare to receive. Challenges remain, but not the old ones. What you gained from past trials and tribulations is now secured in your power bundle, providing the emotional and spiritual skills needed to help you easily hurdle any obstacles you may encounter. Like a cat, you land on your feet, perfectly balanced, standing strong. Now is the time to let go and break free of beliefs about who you're supposed to be. You deserve success and recognition. Relish the feeling.

The Cat Goddess stimulates your natural instincts, making you keenly aware of persons who may not be so happy about your good fortune. Gather those around you who can sustain your success with encouragement and enthusiasm.

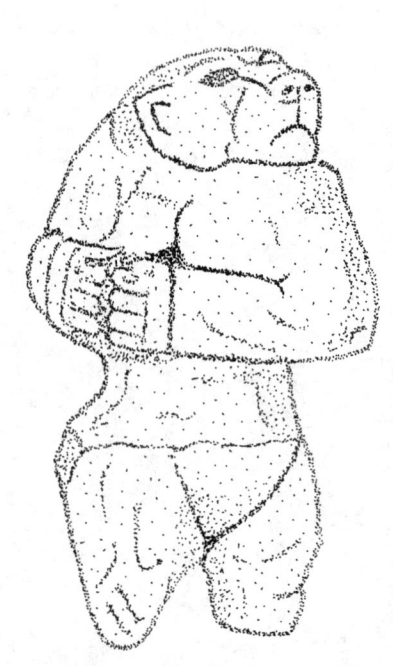

Lion-headed Goddess seems to be "holding tight" while facing a challenge with undaunted courage. Marble. Approximately 5,000 years old, Mesopotamia. (LM)

Goddesses: Bast, Birthing Goddess of Anatolia, Sekmet, Lakshmi, Artemis, Diana.

Qualities To Emulate: Independent, instinctual, playful, self-satisfied, affectionate.

Colors: Yellow, green, gold, silver.

Fragrance: Vetivert (essential oil or dried, ground rootstock).

Creativity/Meditation: "Prosperity Pouch."

Cut a piece of colored cloth four or five inches across in either a circle or square shape. Use any color mentioned above. Anoint the cloth and your Cat Goddess Amulet with oil of vetivert or your favorite fragrance. Place the Amulet in the center of the cloth and breathe deeply in a relaxed way. Concentrate your focus on the Cat image. Envision the good fortune that you want to manifest. See it completed, as clearly and in as much detail as possible. When the image is clear in your mind, imagine green, gold or silver light encircling it, holding it in place, protecting it. Sprinkle a little salt around the Amulet or ground vetivert. Add anything else that might enhance your prosperity

Bast, Mother of all cats, stands as a protectress of Her "litter." She holds a sistrum or rattle in Her right hand and a small cat figure with solar disc and uraeus in Her left. All are symbols of Her sovereign guardianship. 2,600 years old, Egypt. (LM)

The Sacred Animal Amulets: Cat 109

Artemis is associated with Bast, the Cat Goddess. Artemis is the strong and lovely Goddess of the Moon, magic and the lush green forests. She is the archer Who with unerring aim protects women and children, animals and their young. 2,400 years old. (LM)

pouch. Bind the pouch with a silver or gold thread, repeating the following as you tie the knot:

> As I see it
> My fortune grows
> Goodness comes my way
> As I see it
> Guarded strong
> The Goddess makes it stay.

Carry your prosperity pouch with you, helping you retain your vision. When you want to return the Cat Goddess Amulet to your set, replace it with another power object that holds significant value for you. Repeat the binding words as you retie the knot.

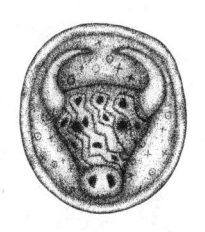

Cow — Uniting in Partnership

The cow personified the Great Creatrix and World Mother everywhere in ancient myth and symbol. Horned, milk-giving and ferociously protective of Her young, the white cow was identified as the Great Moon Goddess. In Irish mythology the cow is a Sky Goddess, Glas Gavlen.[3] In India She is Kali, still considered sacred. In Egypt, She was Hathor, whose udder sprayed the empty night sky with sparkling stars, creating the Milky Way. She gave birth to Her Golden Calf, the sun, each day. Etruscans called Her Lat. Arabs knew Her as Al-Lat and Greeks called Her Io. In Japan the primordial deep went "curdlecurdle" (*koworokoworo*) when the first deities stirred it to create clumps of land.[4] The root of the word "cow" was Sanskrit *gau*, Egyptian *kau*. And the names Gaurie and Kaurie have been used to describe the vulva-like cowrie shell. Her horn, the cornucopia, was the sacred "Horn of Plenty," pouring out the fruits of the earth.[5] The rich diversity of symbolism surrounding the venerable Cow Goddess is imbued with sanctity and respect.

Horned male deities and bull worship were also prevalent in the ancient world, appearing in nearly all religions. Most are adaptations and "reversals" of the original Cow Goddess. Marija Gimbutas claims the bull's prominence is directly linked with the

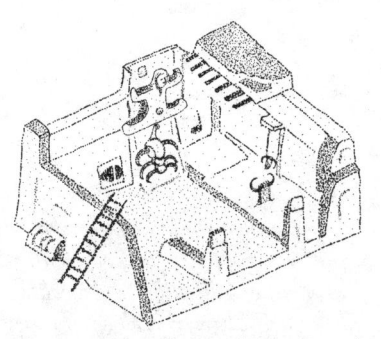

This temple shrine from Çatal Huyuk shows the dynamic forces of "unity" in action. Bulls' heads are placed beneath the birthing Goddess, reiterating a sense of the continuity of life's regenerating forces. (LM)

The Sacred Animal Amulets: Cow 111

Isis leads Queen Nofretari by the hand in sacred union. Isis wears Hathor's horns of consecration. 2,300 years old, Africa. (LM)

In Crete, women and men shared equally in the spiritual sport/entertainment of bull-jumping, working in teams. They trusted each other wholeheartedly with their lives. Bull-jumping was deeply connected to sacred ritual, invoking the divine power of the Goddess to insure the well-being of the community. Knossos fresco. (LM)

Goddess because of the suggested moon symbolism in the horns. The Laussel Goddess with Her moon horn is a Paleolithic representation of this concept. Only later is the bull associated with the Thunder God, masculine power, virility and force.[6]

The image on this Amulet is from Çatal Huyuk. The art and artifacts found there are vivid evidence of the religion of the Goddess, Her symbols, rituals and shrines. Along one of the shrine walls are several life-size bucrania. The overall shapes are made from plaster and painted red. The real horns were pressed into the plaster, and jut out from the walls. "Seats" were built into the floor facing the horned heads, perhaps serving as altars or benches. Horned bull heads and female images giving birth are carved and painted juxtaposed in many of the shrines. Together they depict a complementary play of male and female, a "partnership" of new life emerging.[7]

Çatal Huyuk had no signs of violence or war. Evidence shows that it flourished in peace. I chose this image from Çatal Huyuk because it evokes the potentially beneficent spiritual power of both male and female: Horned Goddess and bull joined in harmonious celebration, the two together sparking new growth.

In *The Chalice and the Blade*, Riane Eisler traces our lost partnership/Goddess societies, symbolized by the chalice, whose love of life, peace, and nature was brutally annihilated by a social system based on the threat of force by male hierarchies, symbolized by the blade. She proposes using the term *gylany* to describe a new model of social structure based on the "linking" of male and female, rather than the "ranking" of the two halves of humanity characteristic of andocratic regimes.[8]

Gylanic models offer hope for our future, viewing partnerships as the sharing of responsibility, living free from fear and the threat of oppression, rape, persecution, and war. Ultimately a gylanic society frees men and women from restrictive and limiting roles imposed by the dominator model. The partnership model is based on prehistoric matristic cultures, emphasizing connecting and cooperation, not material consumption and competition.

When you receive the Horned Cow Amulet it's a sure sign that a partnership is under way. "Connecting" is how we live as social beings. Let yourself enjoy the splendid rush of the experience. As an awakened celebrant you needn't worry about getting "addicted" to the high. Like the Minoan bull jumpers, let the experience be a playful one. If you

In Japanese mythology the male/female deity Dosojin represents the balance and harmony of the male/female forces united as one. (LM)

The Sacred Animal Amulets: Cow 113

feel overpowered in a relationship that seems to re-enact a familiar past scene, find out what role you're playing. Old partnership patterns and behaviors are not easily changed, but once you break them, you can transform your future. When a relationship is developed based on mutual respect by whole and healthy people, a wondrous adventure unfolds. So make sure you're not trying to "fill a space" or distract yourself from some other challenge at hand. Communicate from your heart, speaking with integrity, listening intently. This isn't a performance. You're not an actor performing someone else's script. This is your life; participate in it. Let the Moon Goddess in and share Her gifts.

Whether it's a partnership of lovers, a business association, a creative collaboration, parent and child, or a reunion of soulmates, let the experience enrich your life. The timing is good.

Goddesses: Lat, Hathor, Io, Ninsun, Ninhursag, Au Set, Isis, White Buffalo Woman, Hera, Kuan Yin, Tara.
Qualities To Emulate: Generous, contemplative, wise, protective, compassionate.
Colors: White and black.
Fragrance: Rose (for "heart to heart" communication and openness).
Visualization/Meditation: "A New Vision of Partnerships."

Find a comfortable place to sit. Light a white candle and place it before you. Put a little rose oil on your fingertip and anoint your Amulet, rubbing it slowly, feeling the face, nose, surface texture and curve of the "moon" horns. Continue moving your finger in a clockwise circular motion, "bridging" the space between the horns as you do. Breathe deeply, in rhythm with the "flow" of your finger going round and round. Feeling relaxed and focused, imagine being in a place where all things are possible. How would it feel to be in a partnership in this new place? A partnership without tension, without threat, without force or conformity? What would that partnership be like? How would it feel to honor diversity and equality? What objectives would this partnership propose? How would it be to initiate and cooperate? How would it be to share beauty, peace, creativity, prosperity, love? Let the Cow Goddess tell you how. Remember and write whatever comes up for you. You might try this with your potential partner, each sharing a vision of "partner-shipping."

Dolphin — Joy/Celebration

The word dolphin comes from the word *delphinos*, womb. Delphyne was the Priestess of the Oracle at Delphi and was worshiped as Mother Earth, Mother of the Moon and Sea Goddess in Her various aspects. Her oracular visions and gift of prophecy provided information for communal transition and healing. Her voice was that of the Goddess.

In the Queen's Palace in Knossos on the island of Crete are painted magnificently colored "Dolphin Frescoes." Approximately 8,100 years old, these lively depictions stand as vivid reminders of a culture that reflected the joy of living in the Divine breath and the bounty of the Great Mother. This Neolithic culture reveled in the fruits bestowed on it by Her Earth and Sea, and honored with gratitude the starlit navigational guidance provided by Her Sky.

Life in ancient, matristic Crete was experienced as a joyous wonder, a divine gift. Temples, homes,

The Palace of Minos at Knossos was decorated with lively, fantastical motifs. This beautiful dolphin fresco was painted in the Queen's room along with figures of dancing women and intricate spiral designs on the ceiling — all reflections of life animated with pleasure. (LM)

The Sacred Animal Amulets: Dolphin 115

art, roads, theaters and palaces were all created as innumerable and immeasurable reflections of the joy of living. Walls were decorated with dancing dolphins, laughing monkeys, beautiful flowers and fantastic imaginary creatures. All art was divinely inspired to remind the community of the natural pleasures of life. Strikingly absent from Minoan art are scenes or aggression, war, hunting, or male dominance or violence. All persons enjoyed life equally, sharing in Mother Nature's abundance. This is the spirit of the dolphin.

Aphrodite, Goddess of the Sea, sexuality, and fate, unselfconsciously rides the waves on the back of a dolphin. Pliny, Roman naturalist, said that dolphins loved music and could easily be "charmed" by singing in harmony. (LM)

When you receive the Dolphin Amulet, take a deep breath and dive into the Dolphin Dimension, making merry in a Delphyne Goddess way. She comes to you today for no other reason than to play. In her smiling oracular way she tells you that one of the most profoundly political acts of power is Play (and of course, Self-Love)! Find the laughing place in your heart and let yourself go. Humor has the power to touch your soul, awakening deep, transformative energy. Laugh out loud. Laugh with a friend.

Wherever the Goddess was honored, women enjoyed social, economic and political freedom, sharing wealth equally with men. In Crete, priestesses played the central role in religious rituals and ceremonies. These dancing Cretan women raise their arms in a gesture of blessing. Imagine living in the confidence of a playful spirit. (LM)

The Dolphin Goddess reminds you of the healing power of fun without goal, laughter without reason and joy of simply being. Open fully to this gift of the Delphi. The splendor is all yours.

116 ❧ Amulets of the Goddess

Tune in to the joy of knowing that you are cared for by a loving Divine Creatrix. Delight in the effervescent and extraordinary sweetness of your own being. Let joy resonate deeply from your center, touching all you touch, flowing like a soft wave through your entire body.

Life in ancient Crete was not utopia or fantasy but real, with inherent complications and problems. The Dolphin Amulet reminds you to focus on the joy in your life in spite of real difficulty. Remember that Crete was able to experience a long and joyous existence (approximately 1,500 years) amid male-dominated, warring cultures. When we live our lives creatively and playfully, we are relieved of external directives and trappings. Play alters our perceptions and opens our minds to new possibilities. The solution to a difficult problem is often revealed in reverie or "mind play."

The Dolphin Goddess will help you remember that you are nestled in a glow of wonderment, curiosity, laughter and grace, primal elements of the Dolphin Way. Feel the beauty all around you. Joyous Be.

Goddesses: Aphrodite, Nammu, Mari, all Ocean Goddesses.
Qualities To Emulate: Spontaneous, uninhibited, communicative, peace-loving, playful, nurturing.
Colors: Turquoise blue, green, violet, white-gray.
Fragrances: Gardenia (fresh flowers), water-lily (fresh flowers), orange (essential oil).
Visualization/Meditation: "Dolphin Dancing."

Sit comfortably. Play your favorite meditation music. Anoint your Dolphin Amulet with oil of orange, or have a fresh bouquet of your favorite fragrant flowers before you. Inhale and exhale in long, slow breaths. Become aware of your breathing rhythm, as you bring each breath deeply into your belly. Focus your attention on the dolphin image. Imagine swimming in the warm wonderfulness of a great blue ocean. Imagine that you are a dancing dolphin, smiling and undulating in slippery, deep moistness, your body flowing freely in fluid underwater bliss. You can hear your heartbeat resonating in strong rhythmic pulses. In the primal depths of Earth's living waters, you are an undine, a water sprite, a dolphin, leaping and rolling in funny, friendly frolic. Play is your purpose, and you feel joy in every move, every part of your body.

> Playful watery wondrous
> Dancing Dolphin Divinity
> Float me on Your foamy fun
> Teach me the heart of Joy

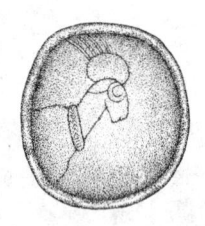

Ewe — Self-Worth

The Sheep Goddess image on this Amulet is based on a prehistoric rock carving found in the Atlas mountains in Algeria (7,000-4,500 B.C.E.), and depicts a scene in which a male figure stands, arms upraised, paying homage before a majestic Sheep Goddess Who wears a radiant disc on Her head indicating Her divinity. Behind Her are two smaller sheep, one wearing the "crown" of radiant energy. The Sheep Goddess also wears a collar with the ubiquitous chevron marks of the Goddess. According to Marija Gimbutas, the chevron is a hieroglyphic sign of the Goddess associated with life-creating and -protecting functions. This ancient image depicts communion with a divine female "source" making Her appearance as a ewe.

The veneration of sacred animals of the Goddess (and most animals in general) was turned around during the patriarchal invasions. The ewe was one of the first domesticated animals to be revered. Before the Great Reversal (sometime during the

Bronze Age) it was the female sheep whose divinity was worshipped, not the Ram and his Golden Fleece. The Sheep Goddess provided wool for weaving, and milk and food for nourishment. Her "creative" and regenerative capabilities sanctioned Her association with other sacred animals, such as the sow, bird and cow, each a manifestation of the Goddess. Animals were considered teachers, friends, and companions. To kill an animal required the sanction of the Divine Creatrix. Complex rituals and prayer for the animal's spirit were performed as part of the sacrifice. The delicate balance of the natural web was understood and honored. Animals have now become force-fed factory commodities, valued only for profit.

Today, calling someone a "sheep" usually refers to a senseless and mindless "follower." Consider the complete reversal that had to take place in the very way that life was perceived in order to change the concept of sheep from divine to "mindless."

I spent some time talking with Kate Treadwell Hill, shepardess at Rutgers University—Cook College. She spoke at length about sheep farming and breeding, which turned out to be a fascinating jaunt into farming and old "country ways." She spoke reverently about sheep. She reminded me of the connection of all nature and animals with the Earth seasons. Prior to forced breeding and controlled birthing cycles, the estrus cycle of ewes in the wild was synchronized with the lengthening of days. The arrival of spring was visible in all forms of nature. And she

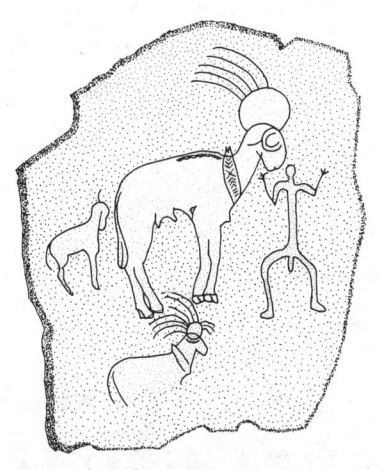

In Algeria this prehistoric rock carving shows a male worshipper in awe and veneration of a Sheep Goddess. Wearing Her radiant "crown" and chevron-etched collar, She is a divine manifestation of numinous life-creating energy. 9,000 years old, Sahara-Atlas Mountains. (LM)

The Sacred Animal Amulets: Ewe 119

summed it all up when she said, "It seems obvious to me why sheep are a much maligned species; they're gentle."

When you receive the Ewe Goddess, it's time to emphasize and encourage the value of your own accomplishments, your own gifts, your own talents. Each person is born with a unique set of variables based on a complex combination of ingredients. Psychological, physical and "cosmic" patterns are woven in a personal tapestry. Get to know the gifts and talents that are uniquely yours and find ways to share them.

In thought, spirit, body, emotion, language and decision, value your personal contribution to the world. Generate feelings of Self-worth by acknowledging that your influence and action have an effect on your environment.

If you're feeling unworthy, find out if you are deferring or giving away power to someone else, perpetuating low self-esteem, feeling helpless and hopeless. If you acknowledge and compliment the talents of everyone else first, take a look at this behavior. Make sure you're not caught in victim consciousness. For women, this attitude is easy to perpetuate since it's been projected onto us for millennia. Practice repeating the profound and empowering mantra "I am." It's as basic and simple an assertion as you can get. And it works. Practice standing and chanting "I am." You'll feel a powerful strength resonating up from your center. And take "action" steps in your daily life to own your personal power.

If you find yourself "mindlessly" following someone else's lead, not able to find your own creative way, take time out for listening to the voice of the Goddess within. The Ewe Goddess, whose wool weaves an infinite array of patterns, reminds you of the endless possibilities waiting to emerge.

Circe, celebrated witch and daughter of Cretan Queen Pasiphae, was a fate-spinner, weaving the destiny of humanity. (LM)

Remember that you can contribute and participate equally without over-doing or over-extending yourself in an effort to "prove" your worthiness. You never have to prove yourself to anyone. Being who you are is enough. In this precious moment your very being radiates excellence.

> There is a woman who weaves the night sky
> See how she spins see her fingers fly
> She stands beside us from beginning to end
> Our grandmother, sister, and friend
> She is the weaver and we are the web
> She is the needle and we are the thread
> She is the weaver and we are the web
> She is the needle and we are the thread.
> —Adele Getty

Goddesses: Ixchel, Tara, Nut, Aditi, Kuan Yin, Arachne, Athena, Moirae, Neith, Penelope, the Valkyries.
Qualities To Emulate: Self-appreciative, gentle, community-minded, resourceful.
Colors: Golden yellow, orange.
Fragrance: Yarrow (essential oil or fresh herb).
Meditation Practice: "Walking With Self-Worth."

Often our posture, how we stand, walk and carry ourselves, is an outward indication of how we value our inner selves, how we embody Self-worth. Be conscious of what your posture and body language are saying about you. Anoint the Ewe Goddess Amulet with Yarrow oil, or your favorite scent. Relax, breathing deeply, inhaling the fragrance. Stand erect with your head and shoulders relaxed, spine straight. Imagine a beam of golden yellow light rising from the center of the Earth, flowing into your body through the soles of your feet. The beam of light surges upward in a long straight line along your spine and pours out the top of your head, making a direct line to the sun. The energy of the golden light is strong and pulls you upward, straightening your spine, helping you stand tall. You feel balanced and centered, your feet firmly on the ground. You are one with the radiant power of the sun and the solid strength of the Earth. You value your skills and talents as a divine expression of these shining and abundant energies. Imagine that you wear a radiant crown, that you are the Goddess. With each step you take, repeat the words "I am."

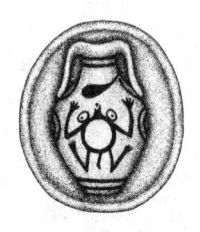

Frog — Speaking Out

The stylized animal image painted on this amphora from early Crete symbolizes the Great Frog Goddess. The amphora was probably used in sacred ritual; it is approximately 2,000 years old.

Both the frog and the vessel are significant, playing prominent roles in the prehistoric language of Goddess cultures. The frog or toad, who visibly and dramatically transforms itself from the underwater silence of a tadpole into a "vocal" amphibian, quite unlike its original form, is analogous to human development from fetus, to birth, to adult human.

The amphora was seen as the active, dynamic female "container," the sacred chalice or cauldron into which cosmic life forces are drawn and from which all life is transformed and birthed. This female-empowering view is unlike patriarchal perceptions of woman as passive receptor. Both frog and vessel are associated with

Frog amulets the world over are associated with power emanating from a female source. Left, frog votive from 19th century Austria. Right, ivory toad carving from Greece, 2,600 years old. (LM)

water, the element of life, and they powerfully resonate and affirm the voice and presence of a Great Creatrix.

Images of frog-women squatting in birth-giving posture, painted on cave walls and carved on bone, are as old as the Upper Paleolithic. In Neolithic art and artifact, the Frog Goddess is rendered and carved in marble, clay and stone.[9] Her presence reinforced a female, body-wise spirituality based on life-giving, healing forces and the sacred blood mysteries of birthing and menstruation.

Frogs were considered sacred to Hekit, the Egyptian "midwife of the gods," corresponding to the Greek Hecate, Crone who stands at the crossroads of life and death. This connection was probably based on the seasonal flooding of the Nile, bringing with it tiny frogs whose presence signified new life about to emerge. As extra protection and guidance for rebirth, frog amulets were placed on mummies. Inscribed on Hekit's "Amulet of the Frog" were the words "I Am the Resurrection."[10]

Frogs were also a favorite familiar of witches. And in many languages the word "toad" means "witch" or "prophetess."[11]

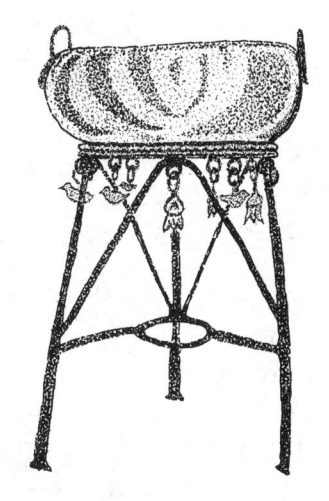

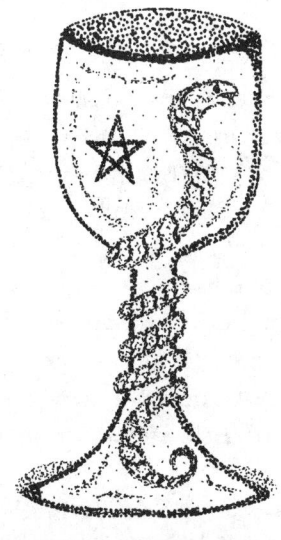

The cauldron, chalice and alchemical retort are magical vessels of transformation. Shamans, priestesses, witches, and queens "mix and stir" their herbs and potions, casting spells, speaking their truths. Above, Great Mother vessel from Greece with bird and bull decorations. Below, contemporary witch's chalice. (LM)

The Sacred Animal Amulets: Frog 123

The body of this Frog Goddess is round, wide and moon-like. The overall spiritual energy of this piece is magnified by the combined symbols that refer to processes of transformation and "becoming." The unconscious vibrates with metaphor upon metaphor of moon, woman, womb, life: She who creates the human world in expressive, cycling, and regenerating patterns.

When you get the Frog Goddess as your guide, it's time to speak up, speak out and express your voice. Who you are and what you say are important. The voice is the soul's vehicle of expression. Words have the power to "move" people, stimulating emotions and thoughts. Your words have the power to ultimately transform your life. And now is the time to say it the way you see it. Don't hold back. A wise woman does not remain silent to protect others' shortcomings. Make waves. Rock the boat. This Amulet represents the vessel of transformation that is initiated by the power of your voice.

Having been silenced by threat of death for so many years, women and "witchy" men have feared speaking out. The Earth calls out to you now. Your voice can heal your heart, heal others and teach the long-silenced language of the Goddess. Tell your story. Let your own voice, your own rhythm fill the world. Speak the words that can set the energy in motion for global change. Risk disapproval. Say the words—make it so. And listen carefully to how the wind brings your rewards back to you.

Goddesses: Hecate, Aphrodite, Danu, The Morrigan, Cerridwen, Nina.
Qualities To Emulate: Articulate, expressive, adaptable.
Colors: Dark green, sky blue.
Fragrance: Sage (burn as incense).
Ritual: "Speaking Her Name."

I gave a presentation recently and before I introduced myself, I stood up and for about fifteen or twenty minutes called out the names of the Goddess in poetic litany, giving meaning to Her name with intonation, pitch and volume. No explanation, no dates, no definitions, no slides. I saw faces smiling and felt the energy surge when women in the audience heard their names or related to certain derivations. The room seemed to vibrate with the ancient sounds, each name invoking and inspiring a vision of a divine female presence.

I recommend this practice as a way of loosening any choking fear that may inhibit vocal expression. Barbara Walker's book *Women's Rituals*, Anne Kent Rush's *Moon Moon* and Patricia Monaghan's *The Book of Goddesses & Heroines* all list the various names of the Goddess from ancient cultures the world over. Whether alone or with friends, stand up and recite Her names. Do it in front of a mirror. Emphasize certain names with firm expression. Use your voice to impart feelings of strength, honor, sensuality, courage, sacredness, joy. Listen to your voice. Speak from the center of your body.

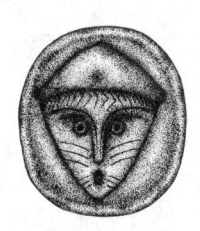

Owl — Wisdom Of The Darkness

Owls are associated with clairvoyance, witches, the Moon, and the wisdom that comes from being able to perceive and speak the truth by "seeing in the dark." The owl is the familiar of many a healer and priestess who channels the mysterious forces of the cosmic, spiritual realm, manifesting the voice of the Goddess through her own, usually under the transformative and guiding light of lunar energies. The owl was sacred to Athena, Greek warrior Goddess of wisdom and the intellect. Lilith, Blodeuwedd, Anath, and other Moon Goddesses, whose clarity of judgement and decisiveness proved important qualities for creating change, all had the owl as their totem or power animal.[12] Many Native American teachers call the owl the Night Eagle. The owl's association with the sacred medicine of the eagle suggests that like the shaman, the owl has the ability to retrieve healing powers from the night world, land of spirits and dreams.

The Bird Goddess in all Her guises is closely associated with water and the watery realm of the emotions. This "bird mask" is carved on the lid of a Neolithic (late sixth millennium B.C.E.) water vessel whose mouth serves as a spout. This vessel, like the priestess, was deemed holy, offering divine effluence. Consecrated and probably used in ritual celebrations, it held the "waters of life," obtained from the rain and the rivers that fed and replenished underground water supplies and sacred wells. The dynamic metaphor that wove the owl, Moon, vessel, water and life with a divine Creatrix bound the emotional energies of the group with the recurring cycles of nature in cosmic harmony.

In ancient times, weather patterns and climatic changes were associated with lunar transformations. Women were the guardians and caretakers of the water supply; the magical art of "rainmaking" was the realm of women in early Greece before the invasions from the north.[13] To this day, my mother will look at the moon and correctly predict rain!

Athena, Goddess of Wisdom, holds Her guardian spirit ally, the owl, as She pours a libation from a vessel. The owl is often painted on her breastplate and shield, and is said to whisper guidance in Her ear. (LM)

If you have called the Owl Goddess as your companion and guide, She will help you see your way through the darkness. If you're up against a wall, She tells you to listen and watch for information that you can't hear with your ears or see with your eyes, information that comes to you by way of your third eye, the eye that sees when your two eyes are closed, your psychic sight. With the Owl Goddess as your Guide you will not be deceived. She will help steer you away from deception or dishonesty. The expression on this owl's face and the one most associated with the owl is "Who?" Is it time for you to ask "Who?" You can move through the darkness with confidence, knowing that inherent wisdom awaits you.

If you have feared the darkness or the unknown, take heart; the Owl Goddess teaches you how to live in the dark while waiting for sunrise. She will teach you discernment in times of doubt. Her power is that of keen perception and unremitting patience. Trust your intuition and psychic "vibes" for instinctual responsiveness. If you're confused or at a loss for words, say, "I'm not sure about what you just said or suggested. I feel a little uncomfortable with it. I'll get back with you after I've had time to

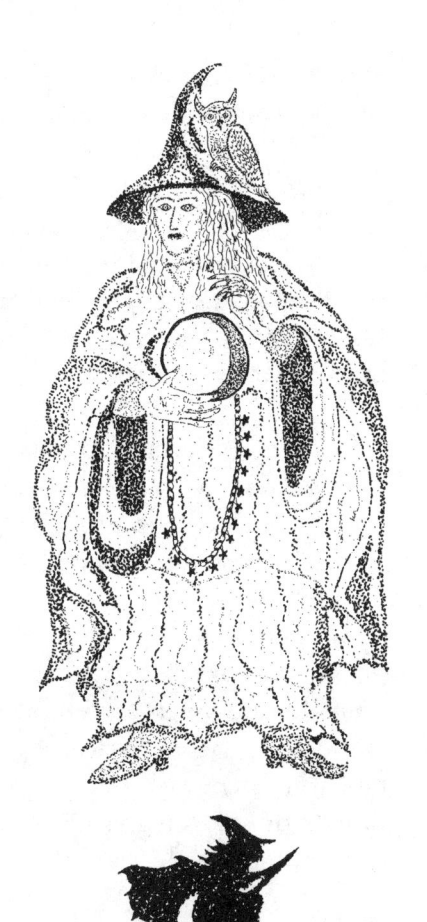

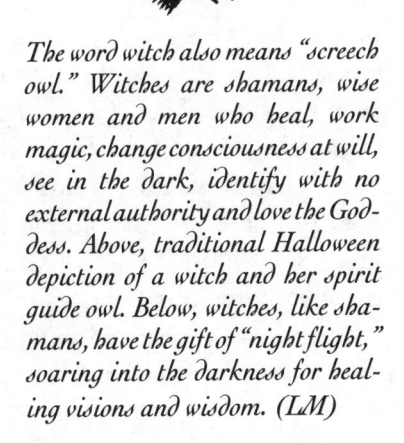

The word witch also means "screech owl." Witches are shamans, wise women and men who heal, work magic, change consciousness at will, see in the dark, identify with no external authority and love the Goddess. Above, traditional Halloween depiction of a witch and her spirit guide owl. Below, witches, like shamans, have the gift of "night flight," soaring into the darkness for healing visions and wisdom. (LM)

The Sacred Animal Amulets: Owl 127

sort it out." And make sure you follow through in your communications, expressing your ultimate decision.

The Owl Goddess knows how to go after what She wants. She also knows what and whom to avoid. She has perfect vision and the gift of flight. She reminds you to "see through" people and situations. Get to the truth. The situation at hand may be emotionally charged, calling for clarity of mind. Use your emotional energy wisely. This Amulet symbolizes the balance of cool intellect and piercing insight.

Goddesses: Sophia, Athena, Lilith, Anath, Rhiannon.
Qualities To Emulate: Perceptive, decisive, wise, intuitive.
Colors: Silver, silvery gray, indigo blue.
Fragrances: Sandalwood (essential oil or incense), eucalyptus (essential oil).
Visualization/Meditation: "Owl Ally."

Give yourself fifteen or twenty minutes of uninterrupted time. Lie down in a comfortable place. Since our bodies are "trained" to associate sleep with a horizontal position, it's important to tell yourself that you're not going to sleep at this time. Since I prefer doing visualization and meditation practice while lying down, I've had to retrain my sleep center, communicating clearly my intent.

Anoint (rub) your Owl Goddess Amulet with oil of sandalwood or eucalyptus, inhaling the fragrance deeply. For this meditation I recommend a hearty, "woodsy" essence. You may want to use incense. Place your Amulet on the space between your eyes, the place of your "third eye." Keep the flat side against your skin. As you breathe, imagine inhaling silvery and sparkling energy through the mouth of the Owl Goddess, bringing that energy all the way to your navel with your breath. As you exhale, imagine sending your breath up through your body, exiting through your "third eye" and the eyes of the Owl Goddess. As you continue breathing and imaging the pathway of your iridescent and silvery breath, your body relaxes. You feel grounded and safe. You feel your body pressing gently against the surface you're on as your muscles soften and you slowly "sink" into it.

Your forehead and the area around your "third eye" relax. You imagine becoming the Owl Goddess. You feel your wings growing wide and strong, your feathers soft and glimmering. Your ears are little feather tufts. Your eyes are golden yellow. You're perched high in a magnificent tree. The sky is indigo blue, deep and quiet. The stars shimmer and shine. The moon is radiantly full. You're able to see far into the distant night. You hear the gentle rushing water of a nearby river. You feel the cool night's breezes against your face. All at once you feel ancient, wise and wondrously alive.

From your place in the tree and with your Owl Goddess eyes, you can see the situation that you're facing. You see yourself wandering in the darkness. You may be lost for words or direction. As the Owl Goddess you are able to see immediately the direction you need to go. You hear exactly what you need to know, listening to your Owl Goddess wisdom.

Whenever you're ready, bring your awareness back to your body. Open your eyes feeling relaxed and refreshed. Carry the Owl Goddess Amulet with you for remembering the wisdom of Her message. Activate practical wisdom.

> I am the wisdom of the Owl and Moon
> Ages and ages old
> I see in the darkest night
> I dwell inside your sight
> I am silvery flowing light
> Ever changing
> Growing bright.

Snake — Shedding Fear, Renewing Hope

This double snake design is from Crete, found on a seal carving approximately 2,000 B.C.E. Throughout Old Europe and the Mediterranean, the snake was revered as a sacred manifestation of the Goddess. But nowhere was the Snake Goddess more prevalent than Crete. With an ability to shed its skin, the snake seemed never to die, becoming a powerful metaphor for the regenerative life force of the Goddess. In several mysterious and beautiful sculptures She is shown with a snake in each hand, often her arms extended by her sides, staring hypnotically and trance-like, a prophetic seer whose vision provides a healing image. One such Snake Goddess is shown with arms outstretched in front and a serpent undulating up one arm, across Her shoulders and down the other arm. Her apron is a "knot" of intertwined snakes. Early priestesses, female shamans of the Goddess, held the primal forces of life and death in their hands.

Serpent deities and creation myths spring forth from every culture. Ananta the Infinite was the serpent mother in Hinduism. She was also Kundalini, primal female energy, coiled at the base of the spine. Through proper meditative practice and yoga, Kundalini energy unwinds, traveling and vibrating through the *chakras*, the energy centers along the spine, unleashing powerful insight and wisdom.

In early Egypt, the Mother of Creation was a serpent. The hieroglyphic sign for Goddess was *uraeus*, snake.[14] The Akkadian Goddess Ninhursag was called Mistress of Serpents, She Who Gives Life to the Dead.[15] In early China, Nu Kua molded humans out of clay, bringing order to the universe. She is depicted as a powerful Goddess, half serpent, half woman.

From the Kulu tribe of northern India a female serpent deity is associated with the rainbow. The rainbow is called Buddh Nagin, "old female snake."[16] Female snake "spirits" are common in Indian myth. In one story, snake maidens rule over the seas. They are energetic, fierce and powerful.[17] The Mother Goddess of early India was never eradicated. She is known as Kalika, without beginning, without end. The Goddess Kali is often shown with a belt or necklace of snakes. She is the creator and destroyer of life; Hers is the ultimate power of transformation.[18]

In the Scandinavian countries, snakes were commonly associated with Goddesses, priestesses, prophets and oracles. On a stone in Sweden, a woman sits in a birth-giving posture, surrounded by a woven snake pattern. She holds a large and winding guardian snake in each hand, the mysterious forces of birth and death interwoven and connected in the magical, female realm.

An Australian aboriginal myth says the Goddess Una created the earth. Sometimes She was pictured as three sisters holding the Rainbow Snake in their arms.[19] A creation myth of the Yaruro people of Venezuela says that Puana the Snake created the world and Kuma, the first person, who established everything that the Yaruro do.[20]

In Native American myth, the

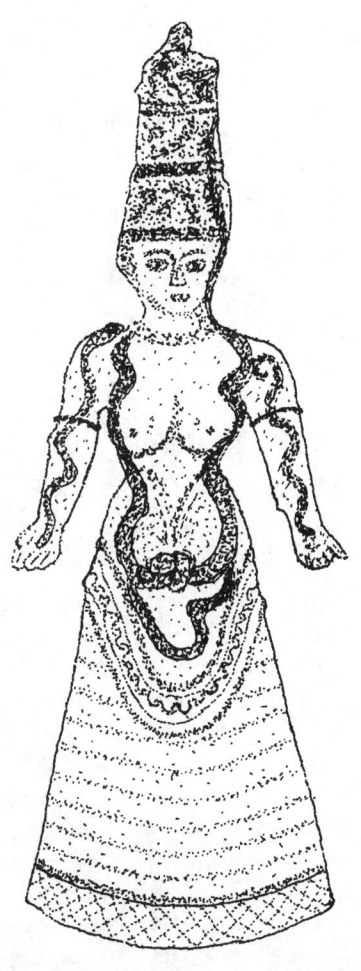

Cretan Snake Goddess stands in hypnotic trance as snakes undulate up Her arms. She is a fearless priestess who embodies the powers of regeneration — letting go of the old, embracing the new. (LM)

The Sacred Animal Amulets: Snake 131

serpent appears again and again. The Hopi perform a "snake dance" each year during the dry season, to bring rain.[21]

The serpent mound of Ohio, winding for over seven hundred feet along the summit of a hill, was built by the Adena and is probably the largest serpent image in the world. The serpent's mystic powers may have provided religious significance to the celebrations and ceremonies performed there.[22]

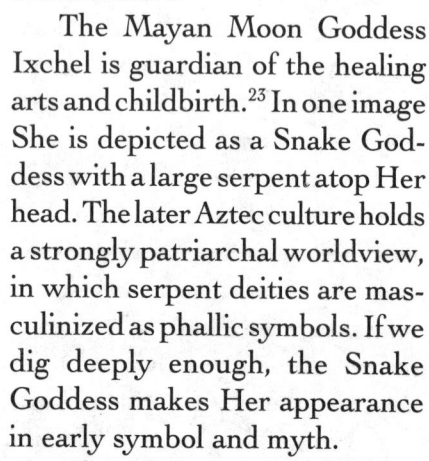

The Mayan Moon Goddess Ixchel is guardian of the healing arts and childbirth.[23] In one image She is depicted as a Snake Goddess with a large serpent atop Her head. The later Aztec culture holds a strongly patriarchal worldview, in which serpent deities are masculinized as phallic symbols. If we dig deeply enough, the Snake Goddess makes Her appearance in early symbol and myth.

After the patriarchal transition, in which the earlier Mother Goddess cultures were overlaid by patriarchal religious and political institutions, the snake was demoted and diabolized, often becoming the "Terrible Mother." The Eden myth tells the story well in which Eve, and inevitably all women, are blamed for the "fall" from Paradise for taking counsel from the serpent, who just so happened to be wrapped around the Tree of Knowledge (Life)! Ironically, the caduceus, the symbol for the medical profession used to

Celtic Snake Goddess sits in childbirth posture surrounded by snakes, symbolizing the magical meandering of life's winding and interconnected "threads." She reweaves and renews the web of life. Above Her head is a knot of three serpents. Knots are frequently used in ritual, spells and incantations; their tying and untying symbolize the binding and unwinding of powerful energy. Because of this, knots are also connected with awakening consciousness, sexuality, marriage, and the shamanic experiences of menstruation, childbirth, and croning. Gotland, Sweden. 1,500 years old. (LM)

132 Amulets of the Goddess

this day, shows two snakes wrapped around a staff.

Everywhere in early myth and cosmogony, the serpent was either the Great Goddess or Her prophetic companion and consort. Powers of life and death and the infinite cycles of regeneration were Her domain. The snake was the personification of living wisdom. With its undulating, swift movement and ability to glide silently and swiftly, shed its skin, "rattle" and deliver a poisonous bite as well as a hypnotic stare, the snake remains a powerful animal "force" in our psyches today.

When you receive the Serpent Goddess Amulet, you are reminded that you carry the wisdom of the Serpent deep in your body and soul. Your memory is alive with "snake power," awakening female transformative energy. You are fierce and fearless. You hear the hissing call of ancient female voices now demanding change, rising up from the "underworld" for the humane treatment of all peoples, all creatures. With the Snake Goddess as your guide, you address all challenges with the desire for personal growth, shedding old fears and repressed feelings, revitalizing dynamic life forces.

The Serpent Goddess often signifies an individual who has faced or is facing her addictions or her past with courage and commitment, living a life fully "awake"

The Hindu tradition says that we are now living in the age of Kali, when the divine female spirit makes Her resurgence. In this sculpture Kali is surrounded by an "aura" of flames and skulls, wearing a serpent-like necklace and headdress, Her daughter seated at Her feet. In Her cosmic dance, Kali reveals the splendor of the female forces of the universe. Stone. India, 16th century. (LM)

The Sacred Animal Amulets: Snake

in the present. You have journeyed to the center of your soul, confronted the "Death Goddess" and wiggled yourself back into the arms of the Great Mother for renewal.

The Snake Goddess reminds you that the process of transformation never ends. The "Death Goddess" or "Dark Goddess" is not the enemy. She was an integrated aspect of the Great Goddess, an inseparable continuum in the never-ending song of birthing, living and dying, until fractured off and relegated to the underworld by androcratic political and religious regimes. In your personal development, She is that part of yourself that you have kept "underground," usually out of fear or shame. She remains potent and charged with anger for having been denied. It may be time to "check in" with the Dark Goddess to see if there's something you've been denying.

In an oppressive patriarchy, we have had to cut ourselves off from the sacred feminine, our "snake power," in order to survive. Both women and men suffer deep psychological depression as a result, not knowing or understanding the value of the darkness. Ultimately, psychic, emotional, spiritual and physical wholeness depend on integrating the lost parts of ourselves. Periodic "dips" into the Underworld for retrieving what may be "dead" or "buried" within us are an important part of the healing process. As that process progresses,

A Nagini is an Indian Serpent Goddess. She has a threefold mission: to prevent access to sacred knowledge to those not deserving; to bestow sacred wisdom on those who are worthy; and to prevent sacred teachings from being lost. Limestone relief, 2,600 years old. (LM)

and the parts are united in oneness, the frequency, duration and intensity of the journey into the Underworld lightens. The journey is often painful and distressing. Without wise and understanding guidance, it can also be dangerous. Personal and planetary survival is tantamount to the integration of our forgotten selves and the reawakening of the Dark Goddess.

When you get the Snake Goddess, it means you understand the importance of allying with what remains hidden.

Goddesses: Shakti, Gorgon, Amazon, Medusa, Kali, Lilith, Ereshkigal, Ua Zit, Fire Woman, Pele, Hella, Coatlicue, Persephone.
Qualities To Emulate: Formidable, uncompromising, clear-sighted, candid, sincere, honest.
Colors: Vibrant reds, including red-oranges, black.
Fragrance: Patchouli.
Creativity/Meditation: "Awakening Serpent Power."

Gather pens, crayons, markers and your journal. Find a photo of yourself, preferably a full shot from head to toe. Use the most recent one you have. You might ask a friend to take some photos of you if you can't find any you want to use. If you go this route, take several different standing "poses" like those of the Snake Goddess as shown. Allow yourself to fully embody Her persona.

Choose a photo you like, letting one "speak" to you. Using scissors, cut away the background image, so that you're left with just your figure. Be careful when trimming around hands and feet.

In your journal trace the Snake Goddess Amulet at the bottom of the page. Glue the photo just above it. Keep a pen close by. Anoint your Snake Goddess Amulet with patchouli oil or a favorite fragrance. Sit quietly, holding your Amulet while looking into your eyes in the photo. Breathe slowly and deeply while relaxing. Imagine receiving the power and wisdom of the Snake Goddess up from your feet, undulating throughout your body. Imagine opening your Self to the sacred knowledge of the

Serpent. What would that feel like in your body? What words would express it? What images? Write or sketch whatever words or images come to mind, placing them all around the photo. Go back to this image or create a new one whenever you receive the Snake Goddess.

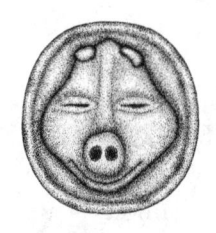

Sow — Listening

The Sow Goddess was honored as a sacred epiphany of the Goddess in the early Neolithic when agriculture was in the hands of women. Her ability to fatten quickly and produce many offspring made for obvious fertility and harvest associations. The pig's ability to root around in the earth was a strong metaphor regarding planting and the "sowing" of seeds. Sculptures of pigs from the Neolithic show indentations where grain was impressed into the wet clay as an act of imitative magic. The Sow Goddess was a seed and vegetation protectress very early on.

This smiling clay pig mask was probably used in sacred ritual honoring the Great Mother. It is approximately 6,500 years old from Macedonia. In Greek and Egyptian ritual, women dressed as sows in celebration of Circe, daughter of Hecate, Goddess of the Crossroads. The Great Mother who gives birth to life eternal through each generation of daughters is powerfully symbolized here and throughout much matristic mythology, embracing the Maiden (Daughter), Mother and Crone (Grandmother) aspects of the Triple Goddess. Ancient Greek shrines show sow-masked dancers wearing "hoof-like" footgear.[24]

Celtic Cerridwen, Syrian Astarte, Egyptian Isis, Greek Demeter, and Freya from northern Europe were all Sow Goddesses, shining white and full like the moon. The bright shining cowrie shell, shaped like a vulva, through which the processes of regeneration took place, was called *porcella* by Romans and from that we get the name porcelain. In Irish the word "pig" is *ork*, the Orkney Islands being sacred to the Crone, or death aspect of the Sow Goddess.[25]

Even today, Tantric Buddhists revere the Goddess as the Diamond Sow, Marici. She is shown seated atop a lotus (womb) throne and drawn by nine pigs. Marici is also known as Sun of Happiness.[26]

The pig played an essential role in two fertility festivities celebrating the Goddess: the Thesmophoria and the Eleusinian Mysteries. The embodiment of the Sow Goddess in ritual and festival magically influenced the possibility of a full, bountiful harvest. In a Lithuanian festival to the Earth Mother the people gather in a circle in the fields, planting egg shells and ham bones to help stimulate abundant growth. Tacitus writes that peoples of the western Baltic region worshipped a Mother Goddess personified as a wild boar and kept boar-shaped amulets and talismans as protection from harm.[27]

Today, small groups of organic farmers are reclaiming exhausted

Isis personified as a Sow Goddess. Here She suckles Her young, her ears drawn back as She remains alert, listening for possible danger. (LM)

Marici-Tara, known as Glorious One, the Diamond Sow, sits on Her lotus (vulva) throne in a chariot drawn by nine pigs. The number nine was sacred throughout the ancient world, representing a triad of the Goddess Trinity. The Muses were the spirit of the Goddess within. Listening to them was a source of inspiration. (LM)

The Sacred Animal Amulets: Sow 137

soil using lunar calendars and elements of "homeopathic" magic, gently nurturing the earth back to fertility with astonishing results. Studies have shown that plants are attuned to the presence of human "vibrations" and respond to a person's intentions accordingly.

The visions we project, both nurturing and otherwise, have a profound effect on our environment. The pig, like so many other animals once revered and held sacred to the Goddess, has been made "lowly" and "unclean." In actuality a pig is very clean in habit. To call a woman a "pig" today is a derogatory term, usually made in reference to her sexuality or body size. During the Great Reversal, what once was sacred has now became "scarred."

When you get the Sow Goddess it's time to put your nose to the ground, "root around" and LISTEN. Listening is a silent act of love, requiring no comments, no defenses. A relationship either with Self or someone else can be fertile ground for personal growth when it is based on deep listening, especially at times when it feels emotionally upsetting or scary. Sometimes the things we don't want to hear are the most painful, yet hold the most healing power.

Open your "psychic ear" and listen to what *isn't* being said. You might be feeling a little confused by "double messages," and the practice of focusing on the "unspoken" or "unspeakable" can help clarify a situation or a conversation, especially if you're dealing with someone who avoids the real issue at hand. It's now time to uncover the real meaning and bring to light something not yet known.

The forest calls back to you the way you call into it. It's important not to confuse this expression with the oversimplified New Age rhetoric that says "we create our own reality," which often, and like the Great Reversal, blames the victim for the crime. The woman or man who was raped as a child did not call out to the rapist. The man or woman who has AIDS did not "ask for it." Certainly, we are responsible for how we experience our reality and our own personal vision of how we work, play, create and participate in it. Individually we are responsible for our health, the jobs we choose, the friends, partners and mates with whom we choose to share our lives. Collectively, there is a mutual responsibility, as well. Wars, pollution, economic instability, violence against women and children, discrimination, inequality and injustice are part of a dis-eased "system" perpetuated by an androcratic and hierarchal worldview. Vicki Noble describes it in *Shakti Woman* as an "invading illness" or a "possessing entity" that has thrown us off balance and separated us from nature. This "entity" appeared some five thousand years ago. The transition from peaceful Goddess culture to sado-ritual domination took us on a serious detour in our evolution, bringing us close to global death. The resurgence of interest in shamanism and the awakening spirit of the Goddess, as well as environmental awareness and other earth-centered and eco-spiritual practices, are now manifesting to "shake off" the possessing entity who has taken over the world. Noble explains that this global recovery movement is similar to a shamanic healing crisis, reclaiming and restoring a state of balance and harmony. If the forests in your mind have been polluted by thoughts and words that denigrate, insult or block new growth, it's time to sort through the debris from the seeds. Find words that truly reflect your heart's intention. Listen carefully to your own language and how you use words to describe yourself, your body, your sexuality, your work, your abilities. What do other people hear you saying about yourself? Reclaim the sacred language and image of this Goddess and listen carefully to Her message. New growth is assured.

> *Goddesses:* Cerridwen, Astarte, Demeter, Persephone, Freya, Marici.
> *Qualities To Emulate:* Fearless, nurturing, loyal, keen.
> *Colors:* White, black, silver, pink.
> *Fragrances:* Cinnamon (crushed sticks), peppermint (fresh leaves or essential oil), lemon (grated rind).
> *Ritual:* "Story Listening."
> It's just as important to listen to someone's story as it is to tell

your own. I have experienced no greater shamanic healing than the simple act of listening, although it's not so simple for Western minds. Listening is a delicate process akin to meditation, creativity, ritual and prayer, requiring that you mobilize your attention and energy for a concentrated effort without goal. Empathy is the healing ingredient and the element that differentiates merely hearing someone from actually listening *with* someone. Empathizing and crying with another person's life heals and makes whole on very deep psychic levels, tapping the sacred "connective tissue" that links us all together as human beings. The "miracle" stories of recovery, hope and healing that I have heard from both women and men sitting in a circle have touched me to my very core. There are very few words to describe the feeling.

Call your friends together. Ask new acquaintances to join you as well. Let them know that you are calling them together for the purpose of "listening." Each person will be telling a little bit about who they are. It may be an incident from the past, a memory, or a reflection about something that is currently happening in their lives. Ask each person to bring a candle.

Sit closely in a circle, a candle in front of each participant. Breathe deeply as if preparing for meditation. Imagine being connected to everyone in the room. Visualize energy flowing from each person in the room into the center of your body. Imagine listening from this place in your center. After a few moments of silence, one by one each storyteller lights their candle, begins with "I remember . . ." and shares a story with the group. Each listener focuses attention on the speaker, listening deeply, without comment or dialogue. The challenge is to listen attentively without thinking about your own story and what you'll be saying when it's your turn. When each person has told a story, close the circle by holding hands, remaining silent for at least three minutes. Share tea or a light snack, holding onto the sacred energy that transpired.

Spider — Sacred Creativity

Here is a carved shelldisk from the Native American Mississippian southern culture in Illinois (original c. 1,000 C.E.). Spider, the Creatrix, sits at the center of Her world, defining Her limits, determining Her own fate, manifesting Her own future.

In many Native American creation myths Spider Woman weaves the world into being. From the Hopi tradition, Spider Woman took Earth and water into Her mouth and created the first beings in order to bring joy into the empty world. Among the Navajo both Spider Woman and Spider Man teach the gift of weaving to their people. Some say Spider Woman wove the web that provided images of the first alphabet. Because She walks on Earth and weaves Her home in the sky, it's said that the spider has the power to bring together two worlds. The Goddess, like the Native American Spider Woman, is said to have initiated creation by first weaving two threads and crossing them at the center of the world, thus creating the four directions. Note that the uppermost body of this Spider Goddess Amulet is divided into four quarters.

In Greek mythology the spider is associated with Arachne, a Libyan princess who learned to weave from Athena. Jealous of her weaving skills, Athena later turned Arachne into a spider. Hence, the word *arachnid*. On a cylinder seal carving from ancient Iraq, a spider protects Inanna's storehouse from insects. In Hindu

A spider protects Inanna's storehouse of grains. From a cylinder seal. 5,900 years old, Iraq. (LM)

myth the spider symbolized the mother aspect of the triple Goddess Maya who spins the Web of Fate.[28]

The spider has been long associated with witchcraft. She weaves her "magical spells" of protection as well as "entrapment" and thereby personifies the Goddess of life and death. Her ability to devour her mate has been the focus of much "arachnaphobia."

Whether spinning tales, casting spells, weaving garments or creating new life from her own body, woman, the Goddess and the spider have always been closely associated, uniting the ethereal threads of cosmic spirits with flesh and blood. In the invisible magic that unites creative vision with action, you'll find the efforts of Spider Woman at work.

Spider Goddess says it's time to weave the sacred dimension of creativity back into your life. Shift gears and experience your own creative world, whether it's art, music, ritual, lovemaking, casting or weaving a spell, dancing, cooking, gardening or writing. She reminds you that sacred dimensions of being are not "out there." The sacred dwells within and waits for you. You don't have to climb the Rockies, trek to Tibet or seek out a guru in Peru. These may be great fun and adventure, but you don't need them for spiritual fulfillment.

The Spider Goddess is the sign of creativity longing for expression. Simple, everyday acts of creativity can bring the sacred into your life for a more sustaining and sensual experience in the now. By focusing your intent and staying present in the moment, making a cup of tea can engender a sense of the divine.

Remember, you don't have to be an artist to be creative, and

Surrounded by seven cosmic hands of creation, Grandmother Spider symbolizes the invisible magic that unites creative vision with action. Shell gorget. 700 years old, Spiro Burial Mound, Oklahoma. (LM)

most likely your "art education" would interfere with the sacred and shamanic dimensions of creativity. It took me considerable effort to dispel the "hex" of art school rules and rhetoric that defined art with narrow, judgmental and scrutinizing eyes. Creativity "experts" say there are many ways to stifle creativity: scrutiny, criticism, competition and grading—all of which are the foundation of most art school programs. When I first began teaching art at a local college, I used creative visualization as a means of introducing each new project. Students were thrilled to be able to access their own imaginations and then manifest their creative fantasies into tangible realities. They were surprised to learn that creativity dwells within, saying "I didn't know I could do that." When word got out about my innovative technique, I was called into the office by my "superiors" to face what felt like the Inquisition. They were concerned that I was practicing some "cult-like religion." Fear of the irrational, creative process is often the most debilitating element.

Creative expression is sacred energy. It is a delicate energy that carries enormous healing properties, evoking the memory, awakening associations long forgotten, stimulating thoughts and activating complex physiological chemistry. It is one of the most important elements in shamanic healing. Let your creativity point you to some new insight.

When you get the Spider as your guide, it may mean you've been thinking about starting a business that weaves your spiritual and creative interests with

Ixchel, Mayan Goddess of creativity, sexuality, prophecy, the healing arts, childbirth and the Moon, sits at Her loom, Her companion bird in front of Her. Did Her animal ally teach Her the weaving arts by building a nest? Ixchel is also personified as a spider who weaves the fate of humanity. 1,200 years old. (LM)

your desire for economic independence. Business can be a powerful agent for creating change, integrating your heart's persona with your role in the world, determining your fate. The Spider Goddess is the symbol of a hard worker who can appreciate the process as much as the product. Go for it.

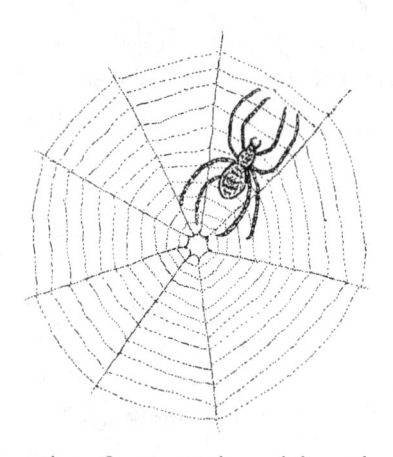

The spider creates her web from the nearly invisible (cosmic) substance of her own body. She decides her fate and that of others by weaving the "world" around her. (LM)

Does something or someone prevent you from feeling creative or welcoming spirituality into your heart? Are you embarrassed about your beliefs? If you feel snared in some unhealthy situation or trapped in some abusive thought pattern and want out, it's time to cast a spell, undoing and "unweaving" it.

Goddesses: Spider Woman, Arachne, Neit, Ariadne, Asintmah, the Fates, Norns, Nerthus, Mawu, Ixchel, Isis, Sunna, Tatsuta-Hime.
Qualities To Emulate: Creative, diligent, intuitive, persistent.
Color: Turquoise blue.
Fragrances: Jasmine (fresh flowers), bay, rosemary (essential oils or fresh herbs).
Ritual: "Casting A Spell For Creativity."

The most important part of any spell, ritual or magic work is your intent and expectation. Focus your intent on what you want to happen and what you expect the results will be, not on what you don't want. You have the power only to change yourself. And you certainly don't want to practice magic that brings harm to anyone. The age-old Wiccan saying still goes, "Do what you will and harm none." You can affect others in mutually respectful ways by changing how you participate or interact with them or by changing your attitude and how you perceive the situation.

State your intention: "I,_____, am casting a spell for getting in touch with my creative Self." Anoint (rub) the Spider Amulet with oil of bay or rosemary. With your hands cupped together, hold the Spider Goddess Amulet, facing out. Focus your breath on Her image, inhaling and exhaling through the center of Her body. Imagine being surrounded in vibrant, turquoise light energy. Imagine sitting at the center of your world, your hands and fingers tingling with creative energy. Imagine spinning your own destiny as a spider spins her web, your hands gathering together creative materials, each strand glistening against the sky, each thread securely woven against the next. As you inhale, draw in expansive, creative energy, filling your whole body. As you exhale, release any unwanted thoughts that inhibit or block creative expression; imagine them carried out on your breath. Continue breathing until you feel full with creative energy. Then say:

> Great Spider Goddess,
> Help me spin creativity into my life.
> Open my soul.
> Let me feel the sacred,
> At the center of my world.
> Move me with your spirit.
> Creative One,
> Help me find my own.
> Woven with the threads of love.
> So be it.

This spell is particularly helpful to those who "buried" their childhood creative curiosity and pursued more "left brain" careers and activities.

The Sacred Symbol Amulets

Comb — Self-Reliance

In ancient cultures the comb evoked vibrant, dynamic energy, stimulating the process of "becoming." Wherever energy is symbolized, the forces of time are indicated.[1] In India and Hopi tribes, the comb represents rain, signaling new growth, fresh life and renewal. The Greek word *kteis* means "vulva" and is often used for the word comb, always a symbol of life-giving power![2]

The comb is also associated with snakes, symbols of regeneration throughout Goddess cultures. Gorgon Goddesses were depicted with heads of snakes, symbolizing their connection to the powerful mysteries of menstruation and renewal.[3] Considering the "posture" of this combination Comb and Goddess, it's apparent that the lines of dynamic energy emanating from between Her legs indicate the activation of life forces.

Since time immemorial, the act of combing one's hair has conjured powerful images of stimulating life energy. A woman's hair was considered a potent ingredient in many a pagan charm, talisman or spell, often an essential element in love potions. According to Tantric wisdom, a woman could activate forces of creation and destruction by braiding and unbraiding her hair.[4] The Catholic Church and Jewish tradition consider women's hair so powerful a force of attraction, temptation and spellmaking

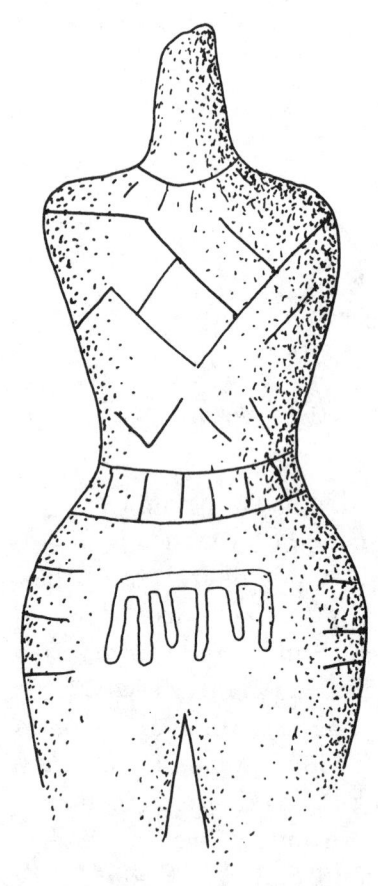

The comb design of this clay Goddess figure symbolizes the activation of life force energy associated with body-based female wisdom, what Emily Culpepper calls gynergy: "the female energy which both comprehends and creates who we are... that impulse in ourselves that has never been processed by the patriarchy..."[6] Clay figure, Moldova. 6,500 years old. (AB)

that religious law insisted women's heads be covered and, in the extreme, shaved.

Fate-spinners and weavers were often portrayed in fairy tales and myths winding the destinies of humanity with threads of hair. Even today European folklore and legend mention the comb as a protective talisman; both children and women wear a comb pendant after childbirth to secure a safe and healthy life.[5]

A baby's brush and comb set is always part of an important "first gift." Like any talisman, a comb or brush is carried almost everywhere: in a purse, in a back pocket, in the glove compartment of a car. There's no denying the trance-invoking meditation of repeatedly brushing one's own hair while gazing into a mirror.

When you receive the Goddess Comb, you are called upon to activate powers of self-reliance. Trust that you alone are the ultimate decision-maker for your life. Listen to the voice within. When you speak, decide and act from personal experience and truth, you set energy in motion. You'll feel alive in your step. When you're in your power, you'll be able to walk into and out of a room without explanation or apology! You won't have to ask permission to be who you are.

Make your decisions yourself, based on your personal truth and experience. At the heart of an inability to decide is often doubt that you have the right to make that decision as it affects your life. If you are looking for someone else to give you approval or make an important decision for you, you are giving away your power about how you should live your life. Author your individual story, creating it as you go along.

When you base your decisions on haste, retreat, fear or desperation, or on someone else's truth or experience, you separate your experience from your essential nature. You'll feel out of sync with who you really are, either racing ahead of your pulse or dragging behind it.

Practice merging with your pace and the Goddess energies within. Focus on your body in this very moment. Check in periodically throughout the day to find out what's going on in your body. What does it tell you? The point of personal power is that you can trust the experience of the bodily moment. For example, how many times have you walked away from a situation where everything in your body was screaming "No!" and your mind was repeating "Oh, it's really OK"? Moments or even days later, you wake up fuming

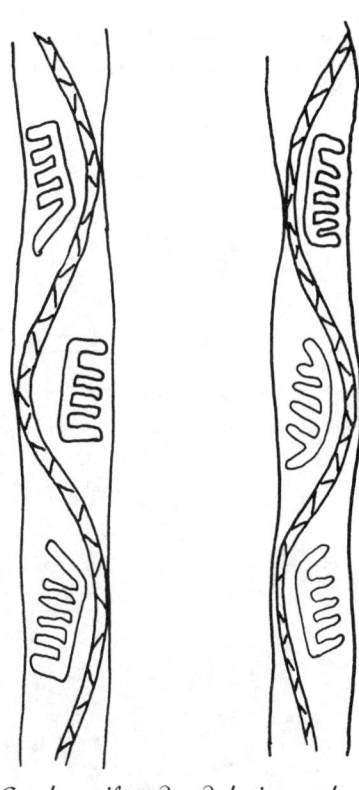

Comb motifs and undulating snake patterns carved on Upper Paleolithic bone ritual implements and tools suggest that the carrier/user was in contact with the divine. Dordogne, France, 15,000 years old. (AB)

The Sacred Symbol Amulets: Comb

and frustrated, realizing that you were in two different places at once, manipulated or disempowered.

When you are truly comfortable in your body and the rhythm of your life, you can acknowledge and respond from that inner place that always has your best interests at heart. Each time you merge with your pulse, listening to and acting on your innate wisdom, you strengthen your self-image.

Rely on your body's psychic information to know what feels right and wrong. Rely on the wisdom that teaches patience; let truth reveal itself. While some decisions can be made in a split second, delaying decisions while waiting for more information can be a wise decision in itself. When you listen to your body, you'll know when you know. Information does not equal transformation, but it is the first seed of the harvest and the first step toward a new vision.

If you disregard your body's subtle signals, and you don't pay attention until you're hurting with headaches, exhaustion, irritability, aches and pains, stay "in tune" to keep in harmony and health. In order to use body-based wisdom, you have to learn to recognize it.

Aphrodite, self-defining, self-reliant, activating elemental forces of self-love, creativity and self-assertion. In this image, Aphrodite seems to be "letting Her hair down" while bathing in the ocean — the primordial Mother Element. (LM)

Goddesses: Athena, Brigit, Cerridwen, Ganga, Sarah, Sarasvati, Shakti, Fuji, Aphrodite.
Gather Images That Evoke: Self-assuredness, confidence, good health.
Colors: Yellow, orange, red.
Fragrance: Ginger (fresh

root or essential oil).

Meditation: Pendulum.

Using a pendulum is an excellent way of contacting Goddess energies, helping you rely on your inner resources for making decisions. I bought my first pendulum on a whim and I've used it daily ever since. It sits on my desk, within reach for consulting whenever needed. Sometimes when I'm conducting business over the phone, I use my pendulum to "pick up the vibes" of the transaction. I've gotten some surprisingly accurate responses!

You can easily make a pendulum by tying a chain or a heavy thread around a crystal or weighted object such as a pendant or earring. Mine is very simple, made of brass with an eight-inch chain and a bead on the holding end.

Grate some fresh ginger root and inhale the fragrance before beginning, or use a drop of ginger oil to lightly anoint both your Amulet and pendulum, focusing on your intention. Sit comfortably with your pendulum in your writing hand, holding it over the Comb Amulet in the other. Hold the end of the chain or thread with your thumb and one other finger. Relax, breathing long, slow breaths. To get acquainted with your pendulum's personal signals, ask for a "no" and then a "yes" response. My pendulum responds very clearly. "Yes" is up and down. "No" is left to right. "Maybe" or "indecisive" is a hovering vibration, without movement. You may get circular motion for "yes" or "no." When you're familiar with the way your pendulum responds, ask a simple yes-or-no question, while focusing on the image of the Comb Amulet. Detach emotionally from the question and the outcome. Let the Goddess energy within guide you.

Note your experiences in your journal.

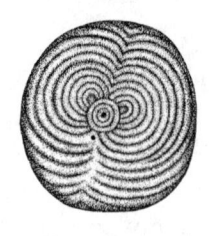

Eyes — Reflecting Inner Visions

From a shrine chamber in Sess Kilgreen (County Tyrone, Ireland, 3,000 B.C.E.), this sacred symbol of the Goddess represents Her omniscience. Concentric semicircles flowing out in wavelike rhythm from the center act as a mandala. It is illuminated by the sun at Summer Solstice, a time of accelerated growth and fruition.

Imagery that focuses attention, de-emphasizes left brain activity and opens the way to intuition has been used for oracular and divination purposes through the ages. Meeting our Divine Source teaches us inner vision.

Eye Goddesses and the association of a beneficent Source with the eye motif have their origins as early as Paleolithic times. The Dolni Goddess, 24,000 B.C.E., has incised markings from eyes to breast, symbolizing streaming moisture and strongly suggesting the Goddess as all-seeing. Entrances to tombs and temples on Malta and Sicily were carved with double spiral eye designs. Participants in Her celebrations and rites were guided through the gates by Her wise gaze. During Neolithic times, pottery vases, lidded jars,

Eye Goddess protecting smaller inner child Goddess. Her eyes reflect on the outside what she knows to be true on the inside, creating a divine union like that of Mother and Child — creator and created. Clay. Syria, 5,000 years old. (AB)

152 ❦ *Amulets of the Goddess*

masks and bone amulets were carved and decorated with vibrantly painted eye motifs and probably used during sacred rituals.[7] The Eyes of the Goddess are associated with the Bird Goddess, in particular the owl. The wisdom of the owl has survived to the present day in art, myth and folklore.

The blessed Eyes of the Goddess became the "evil eye" under patriarchal rule, when men projected their fears onto women, nature and the ancient religion of the Goddess. Each Goddess attribute was splintered from beliefs and practices. For example, women, especially older, postmenopausal women (Wise Crones) were ordered to keep their heads bowed and their eyes lowered in the presence of men, lest they cast an evil spell with a direct glance.[8]

The Eyes of the Goddess predict a deep and heartfelt transformation in your perception of relationships. Whether it's with yourself, family, lovers, friends, peers or your environment, replace projection with vision. If your view of the world has been blinded by fear, distrust or scarcity, use your imagination to replace old, self-

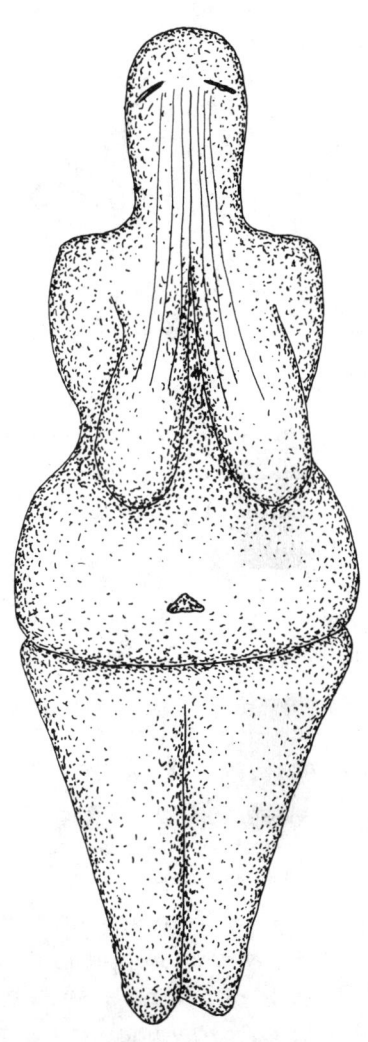

Dolni Goddess, Whose eyes and breasts are connected by incised lines, suggesting divine moisture and the Goddess as all-seeing. I think of this image today as "the eyes seeing what the heart beholds." Clay. 27,000 years old, Czechoslovakia. (AB)

The Sacred Symbol Amulets: Eyes 153

defeating and self-limiting illusions. Imagine seeing the world through the eyes of a child.

Carry the Eyes of the Goddess with you to know the way it *can* be. Patriarchal institutions thrive on helplessness and despair. Let your Goddess Guides show you the world through the perspective of "fullness," reflecting and acting on a picture of wholeness and holiness. Observe and trust the stillness. Learn by watching the trees grow. Listen to the wise woman within. She is your witness. You may have to take another path. The one you're contemplating may be attractive for all the wrong reasons. The unknown is frightening. Compulsive action is often mindless. Look into the eyes of love. There is a reward for waiting. It may slow you momentarily but will focus your intent and purposes. Like Artemis, do not release the arrow until you are sure of your target.

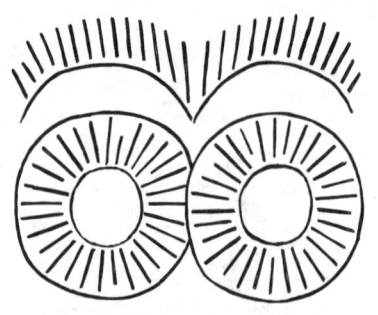

Radiant wisdom emanating from the eyes of the Goddess. From a ceramic cup, 5,000 years old. Spain. (AB)

Goddesses: Amaterasu, Circe, Freya, Isis, Morrigan, Tlazolteotl, Uzume, Artemis.

Gather Images That Evoke: Clarity, trust, self-confidence, satisfaction, awe.

Colors: Clear, sparkling blue, iridescent purple.

Fragrances: Peppermint (essential oil or fresh leaves), coffee (ground beans), caraway (ground seeds).

Visualization/Meditation: Transforming Relationships.

Sit comfortably. Light a candle. Breathe deeply, inhaling one of the fragrances above. Hold the Eyes of the Goddess Amulet in your hand. Gaze into the pattern of lines. See in your mind's eye the person or situation with whom you want a different relationship. Imagine a conversation or an activity with this person, place or issue. Focus on how it *could* be different. Imagine a clear blue energy field, sparkling and iridescent, surrounding you. Sense the loving eyes of the Goddess on you, watching with tender, loving care.

Write your experiences in your journal.

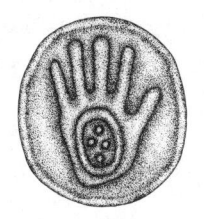

Hand With Seeds — Accepting Responsibility

The Neolithic village of Çatal Huyuk, in present-day western Turkey, is approximately 9,000 years old. It was dedicated to the Great Mother. Built over a sacred well, it encompassed 30-35 acres; thus far, up to twelve layers of structures have been excavated. A ceremonial center, Çatal Huyuk was apparently located on a busy trade route for obsidian, grains and perhaps Goddess figurines and amulets.

James Mellaart's archaeological excavations there revealed an enormous wealth of information regarding this most famous Goddess site. Although his research was curtailed when the Turkish authorities put a halt to his expedition, he was able to determine that the Goddess was the focal point of the village's religious rituals and symbolism. The inhabitants were peaceful agrarians.

Painted and carved murals of ritual scenes and sacred images abound within the temple walls. The Goddess appears for the first time in Her triple aspect of life-giver, nourisher and death-wielder, represented in paintings and reliefs. The hand motif is found in many of the site's shrines associated with bull heads (perhaps horned cows), painted in the colors of life (red) and fertility (black).[9] A familiar image, the handprint was used throughout Paleolithic cave drawings. The laying on of hands is the use of healing touch, generating and directing life-force energy through the hands.

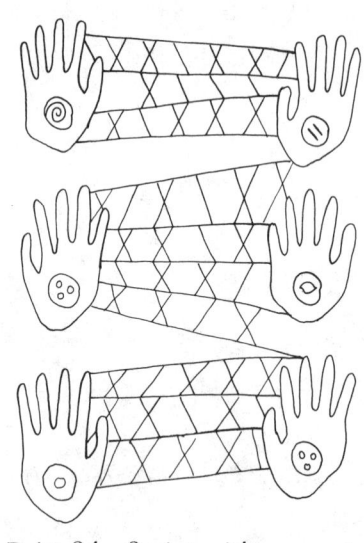

All the handprints on one particular wall at Çatal Huyuk are shown with an open area in the palm. Some palms have circles or clusters of dots drawn in the center. Are these the seeds of growth, the eggs that carry life? Do the handprints honor the presence of the Goddess? We can only imagine.

Painted handprints with woven net-like honeycomb design from a shrine wall at Çatal Huyuk, divine energy emanating from the hands of the Goddess indicating action and protection. (AB)

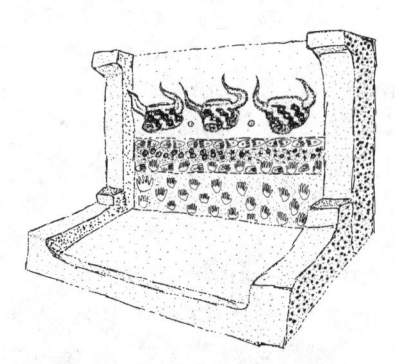

The seeds of growth are in your hands. It's not necessary to invent the seeds, but you have to nurture them. When you receive the Seed Hand Amulet, you are asked to take responsibility for what belongs to you. If you've been moaning about being in the "pits," the Goddess reminds you not to throw them away. Plant them. Water them. Nourish them. Watch them grow. With enough patience and love, you'll have your own Tree of Life. Request a helping hand if you need one.

No matter what discomfort you may be feeling, whether it revolves around issues at work, home, or in relationships, the seed that germinates new growth will be found somewhere near the discomfort. In nature, the cure for

Handprints and horned skulls create a sacred shrine at Çatal Huyuk. What ceremonies and rituals were performed there, we can only imagine. The presence of the Goddess was certainly invoked. (LM)

poison ivy, jewel weed, is often found within ten feet of the plant. Susun Weed says that poison ivy grows to protect once-devastated land. Whatever inspires you to walk in the woods in the first place will reveal an important clue. An antidote is within reach. The gift of discomfort is to be able to identify its source. Find out all the things that make you "itch." Be willing to let them go with compassion. Invoke the presence of Kuan Yin for comfort. It's the best that you can do. The responsibility for your health is in your own hands. In times of discomfort, make the promise not to abandon yourself.

A prehistoric cave painting shows an entire wall covered with hundreds of handprints in green, red, blue, black, and white. Their rhythmic pattern seems to come alive, emphasizing a sacred place and the presence of a divine force received and transmitted by the hand. Cueva de las Manos, Argentina. (LM)

If you've spent an inordinate amount of time protecting and holding onto your seeds, now is the time to plant them, letting them go and letting them grow. If you've held yourself back for some reason, your Goddess Guide now whispers a wholehearted "Yes." This is the planting season. Start something new: friendships, creative projects, gardening, classes, workshops, a spirituality or recovery group. Or take the first step toward a more fulfilling career.

The essential wisdom of this Amulet is: Pray for corn, but first plant the seeds.

Goddesses: Demeter, Ceres, Viking Norns, Tara, Kuan Yin, Ops.
Gather Images That Evoke: Strength, vitality, courage, hope.
Colors: Pearly white, green.
Fragrances: Cinnamon (crushed sticks), nutmeg (ground seeds).
Visualization/Meditation: Seeds of Responsibility.

Sit quietly and comfortably. Inhale one of the suggested fragrances, bringing the aroma deep into the center of your body with long, slow breaths. Imagine that you hold four seeds in your left hand. Each seed represents something in your life for which you alone are responsible. For instance, one seed might represent your responsibility to eat healthy foods, the next to ask for comforting. Perhaps another signifies your need to find a rewarding and satisfying job.

Focus your attention on the seeds, each one vibrant and alive with possibilities for growth. Imagine being drawn to one of the seeds: one that needs your attention. Let it call out to you. Visualize planting it. Feel the satisfaction in self-fulfillment. What are the fruits of your endeavors?

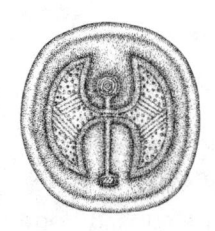

Labrys — Priestess Power

This image is from a Minoan vase, 1,600 B.C.E. The labrys, or double-bladed axe, is a symbol of the ancient Amazon tribes of Asia, North Africa, Anatolia and the Black Sea area. They were women who lived together, celebrated the Goddess in nature and all life and fought to preserve their matrifocal culture against the invading patriarchal forces. They governed and supported themselves and enjoyed art, poetry, athletic games and numerous crafts, as evidenced in story and artifact. They have been portrayed as ferocious, courageous, beautiful, strong leaders. Legends say that the Libyan Amazons were the first to tame wild horses.[10] Although they are considered mythical, the evidence for their existence is too convincing to be ignored.

Amazon tribes settled and lived in Cappadocia, Samothrace

and Lesbos, and founded other Goddess centers, according to Greek myths—Smyrna, Ephesus, Cyumes, Myrine and Paphos. These centers flourished for centuries, even millennia, under matriarchy.[11] Amazons were priestesses of Artemis, the Moon Goddess. At Ephesus, a great temple was built in Her honor. Medusa, serpent-headed Libyan priestess, was a well-known Amazon. The Greeks feared her tremendous power. The myth of Perseus slaying Medusa symbolizes how "heroic" invaders vanquished the Amazons by the sword and gradually reduced female power and Goddess cultures.

Butterfly-like, the labrys is also a symbol of regeneration and the powers of life that unfold and renew themselves from what has passed. The magical transformation from death to life was always in the hands of the Goddess and Her priestesses.

When you receive the Labrys Amulet you are ready to accept and embody priestess power. You stand strong, arms outstretched, "winged," receiving and transmitting Her messages with divine clarity. Your energy is focused. You are now more in touch with your psychic awareness than ever before. You trust "process" and the truth of your personal experience. As a benevolent priestess, you are keenly observant and see beauty even in the midst of decay. You acknowledge the natural cycles of life and death as a continuum in the Great Round—Goddess as Source. You understand the spiritual concept of "balance," which involves constant, unified movement; without movement, life becomes static and stagnant.

Priestess from Crete holds a labrys in each hand. Her arms are uplifted in a gesture that signifies her powers and abilities to "draw down" lunar energy and administer the transformative energy of the Goddess. (AB)

The Sacred Symbol Amulets: Labyris 159

The Labrys is a symbol of your matriarchal heritage. In the face of authority, you hold your ground, supporting radical changes for a clean environment, better health care, child care and elder care. You know that your decisions, not conditions, shape your destiny.

Accepting Priestess power includes radical truth-telling and dangerous innovation. This often means confronting situations, personal as well as political, as a fearless and formidable visionary and facilitator of change, using words, thoughts and creative expressions that the dominant authorities consider unimaginable or unthinkable.

Your enthusiasm is contagious. You remember and cherish a time when all people lived in peace and you envision a peaceful future today, initiating rituals and celebrations to help others remember, too. Goddess consciousness fills your heart and guides your imagination.

Minoan urn, elaborately decorated with life-affirming symbols of Moon, labrys, plant and cosmic spirals, represents the natural cycles of old-becoming-new, a process in which all life participates. Crete. (AB)

Goddesses: Cretan Snake Goddesses, Amazons, Deborah, Nanshe, Harmonia, Ishtar, Maat, Cybele, Artemis, Athena, Queen Kleite, Hippolyta, Antiope.
Images: Ancient priestesses, women leaders, heroines.
Color: Purple.
Fragrances: Patchouli (essential oil), frankincense (essential oil or incense).
Ritual Celebration: Priestess Party.

When you get the Labrys, it's

time to celebrate and honor ancient priestesses. Decorate your "temple" with draped cloth everywhere (use bedsheets and scarves). Send invitations to your dearest friends, asking them to come dressed as their favorite priestess of the Goddess. Norma Lorre Goodrich's book *Priestesses* is a perfect source for inspiration.[12] Ask them to bring a dish to pass around, special food fit for Her divine emissaries. No junk food! Light candles. Play sensual sacred music; I recommend Layne Redmond's ritual drumming tape *Since the Beginning.*

When everyone arrives, stand in a circle. Each Priestess anoints the next with patchouli oil (or her favorite essential oil), rubbing a small amount in a spiral on her forehead as she says, "You are sacred. You are special. You are a wise, wise woman." Feel free to improvise, re-creating it differently each time. Pass the Labrys Amulet. Ask each priestess to introduce herself as she receives the Amulet. Encourage her to speak her "prophecy," telling everyone how it was during her time and what she foresees for a Goddess future. Close with the following chant:

> We are One with the Goddess divine.
> We are the priestesses of ancient Mother time.
> We know in our hearts Her story is true.
> We are here to celebrate and share it with you.

Dance to some great dance tunes and share food.

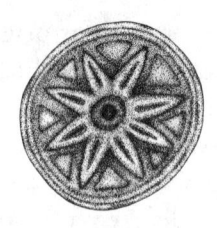

Nightstar — Fulfillment

This image is from a Minoan seal impression approximately 4,000 years old. To ancient matristic cultures, the night sky was the realm of the Goddess. As Morning Star, Evening Star, Astarte, Stella Maris, Venus, Isis, Nut and Hathor, She was guardian and sovereign of the living Sky. In Her many Sky aspects She was breathing, living light, birth-giver of the universe and receiver of the souls of the dead. As Nut, She took the form of the Cow Goddess Hathor, Who created the Milky Way.

She was also pictured as Queen of Heaven, Her long body arching over the Earth from horizon to horizon. She wrapped Herself around the living in a gesture of caring protection and absorbed the dead back into Her body.

Nut, Matrix of the Universe, arches over an image of Hathor, honoring Her as the celestial Cow Goddess. The stars light up the sky behind them. In Egypt, women were called nutrit, *little Goddess. Painted ceiling, Temple of Hathor, Denderah, 2,100 years old. (LM)*

When you get the Nightstar Amulet, the Goddess is beckoning you to rejoice in ultimate personal fulfillment. As Starhawk's version of the traditional *Charge of the Star Goddess* says, "Let there be beauty and strength, power and compassion, honor and humility, mirth and reverence within you."[13] You feel blessed in Goddess delight. Open fully to the experience.

When you wish upon a star,

your dreams come true—and that star is you! So make your wishes. Include prayer in your everyday activities, touching on Goddess energy, awakening Her illuminating brilliance within. I have recently awakened to the power of prayer in my own life. As a child I said my prayers before going to bed every night, racing through a silent Hail Mary and Our Father that if spoken out loud would sound like incoherent gibberish. I never thought about the words and wasn't interested in them. The only part that slowed me down was the last sentence which I spoke from my heart: "Bless Mommy, Daddy, my brothers, me, and the whole wide world." That alone seemed like the biggest wish I could ever hope to see come true. Now I say my prayers slowly, thoughtfully, reverently and with love. I know the power of "the word" and the magic of living life fully attuned to the benevolent graces of the Goddess.

Universal energies are at your command now. This is a perfect time for casting spells, personal or group ritual work, celebration, shamanic trance work, creativity, getting your astrology chart or your palm read, or experimenting with various healing techniques such as laying on of hands, aura reading, pendulum work and geomancy. Remember that the Goddess speaks through you. Keeping this in mind, you won't get caught in a self-righteous ego game.

You are fulfilling your purpose under the radiant light of a nightime star.

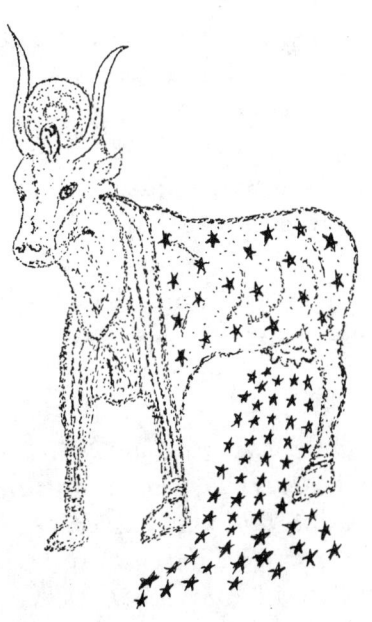

Hathor, Star Queen and Goddess of the Night Sky, giving birth to the Milky Way from Her sacred body. (LM)

Goddesses: Isis, Nut, Hathor, Amaterasu, Cassiopeia,

The Sacred Symbol Amulets: Nightstar 163

Esther, Mayi-Mayi, Pleiades (Seven Sister Stars), Astarte, Stella Maris, Venus.

Gather Images That Evoke: Your heartfelt desires, good omens, optimism, paradise.

Colors: Midnight blue, silver, deep purple.

Fragrances: Myrrh (essential oil), juniper (essential oil or incense).

Visualization/Meditation: Star Gazing.

On a warm evening spend some time gazing into the night sky. If you feel inclined to get to know the constellations, bring a star map. Set up a little outdoor altar to the cosmos and the constellations. Bring incense, a candle, your favorite Goddess figurines or images, crystals, and a blanket to lie on. Lie on your back and relax, inhaling one of the fragrances suggested above or one of your own favorites. Hold the Nightstar Amulet in your left hand, your right hand over your heart. Breathe deeply while gazing into the infinite darkness and the stellar energy of the Goddess. Reach with your left hand toward a star that attracts you. Imagine receiving star energy through your hand, channeling it into your body. When you feel your energy heightened, make a wish, squeezing the Nightstar Amulet tightly. Try this meditation when the Moon is full and during the Dark Moon.

This is also a fun way to spend an evening with friends. August is the month of the "shooting stars." Lie in a circle with heads together in the hub; each time someone sights a shooting star, they call out one wish for themselves and one for the world.

I am wishing on a Star touching the indigo underbelly of the Night sky cave bowl. Sparkling points of fire pierce holes through Her evening cloak. I am wishing from afar, reaching, stretching, charting my course in the Silver Wheel — Celestial Goddess of the living fire map. My skin on the sky, my hands palm up touching each star as She carries me on Her back in Her chariot.

We are riding fast, skipping freely. Infinite possibilities beckon my passage. I am returning, burning bright and twinkling. I am a luminous thread. I am a star seed of Her majestic Milky Way. I see in the divine darkness of my own cosmic dark nest. I am lovingly, longingly unfolding with each night and light breath. I am Nightstar and Sky Queen in the Galaxy of the Goddess and I am carrying Her Nightsongs into daybreak.

Sprouting Seed — New Beginnings

The Sprouting Seed image is from a Cretan seal. The original is approximately 4,000 years old. Seals were used throughout Crete as "stamps." Each seal's image was pressed into wet clay or wax, assigning meaning to the item. Some may have related to seasonal festivities and celebrations. Images and symbols that spoke of the energies of Nature were used on ritual and ceremonial vessels. Other seals were used in agriculture and trade, identifying grains, oils, flours and precious stones.

Seed and plant images provided powerful associations with the promise of growth and life. Vulvas and plants are closely associated, appearing in stone, bone, and clay carvings throughout Old Europe.[14] Birth and regeneration are closely connected to the Goddess, Nature and female energies. In many countries up to this century, peasant women exposed their genitals to flax plants and prayed to the new growth in hopes that the plants would grow as high as their genitals.[15]

When you receive the Sprouting Seed Amulet, a tender and vulnerable situation may be at hand. It signals the beginning of something new. You've already planted your "seeds" and taken conscious care to give them a healthy environment. They are growing beautifully, unfolding with the love you have provided. During this stage of growth, balance is the best care. Concentrate on "rootedness." Establish your foundations so that whatever you build upon them becomes a strong and steady home in which to dwell.

At this time, review your goals and expectations regarding the outcome of your wishes. Toss out what isn't relevant anymore. It's important to make revisions along the way. You can't tug at your plants to make them grow. When you can trust the mystery that underlies patience *and* persistence, a strong and healthy outcome is certainly in store.

Goddesses: Flora, Demeter, Pandora, Hebe, Lakshmi, Venus, Zemina.

Gather Images That Evoke: Strong new beginnings, healthy growth, prosperity.

Color: Green.

Fragrances: Spearmint, peppermint, lemon balm (fresh leaves or essential oil).

Ritual: New Beginnings.

When you receive the Sprouting Seed Amulet it's time to affirm your commitment to a growth process that you began a while ago. Call together a few of your closest friends, especially those who are aware of current issues in your life. Ask them to bring a passage to read that honors your personal growth process. It can

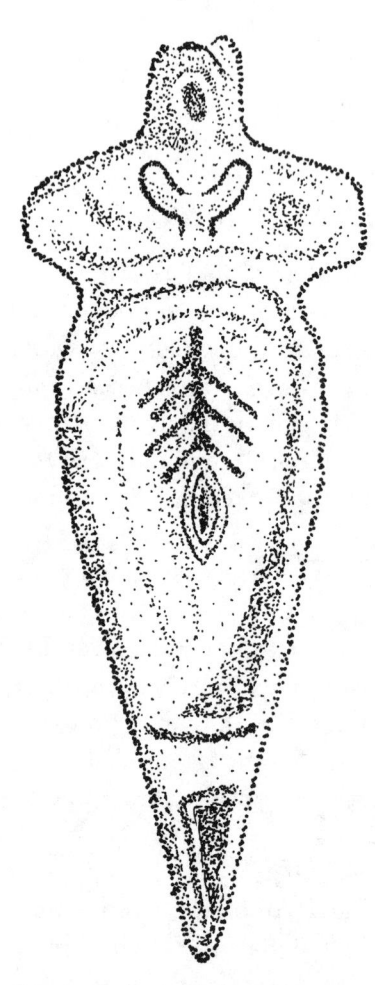

Image of the vulva and sprouting seed motif on Goddess carving. The seeds of a new beginning germinate within. Neolithic Italy. (AB)

be something they wrote. Use a green or floral printed cloth or sheet on the floor to establish your ritual space. Place a potted plant in the center. You may want to bring a new one into your home as a visible reminder that you are watching something grow. I have two plants in particular that have been growing with me over the past decade. They respond to my affections and attentions almost immediately. Taking care of them helps me focus my energy, reminding me of how the process works: with tender loving care.

Arrange your favorite stones, talismans, jewelry or Goddess images around the plant. Bring to the circle whatever has meaning for you. Fill a pitcher with water, put a long-handled wooden spoon or "stir stick" in it and place it in front of you. When everyone is seated, light a green candle. Anoint the Amulet with oil of peppermint. As you do, ask the group for their support, saying something like "I've called together the wise women in my life to help me remember how to grow; to encourage the processes of change in my life; to stand with me when I face my fears; to honor each fragile new step as I take it, and to help me celebrate each step of the way with love. I welcome your support for_____."
At this time, stir the water in the pitcher, saying "And I stir the nourishing waters of life to make it so."

Pass the pitcher of water and the Sprouting Seed Amulet to your left. As your friend reads her passage to you, she holds the Amulet out in front of her in your direction, in your honor. When she finishes reading she stirs the pitcher, repeating, "And I stir the nourishing waters of life to make it so." Each woman in turn does the same. When the pitcher and Amulet return to you, complete

The miraculous journey from a tender beginning to rooted, mature growth is one of trust and patience. Much of a plant's tender beginnings are spent in darkness, preparing and strengthening the roots that will eventually provide nutrients for aboveground growth. (LM)

The Sacred Symbol Amulets: Sprouting Seed 167

the ritual by pouring a glass of water from the pitcher and drinking half a glass. Water the plant with the rest. The women in the circle clap loudly and exuberantly, instilling the air with vibrations for a new cycle of life beginning.

Share food and exchange words of encouragement.

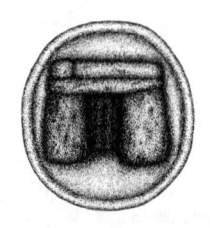

Temple — Breakthrough, Awakening, Healing

The island of Malta, in the Mediterranean between Libya and Sicily, is home to some of the oldest and most impressive megalithic Goddess temples. Little is known about the people who lived there between 5,000 and 2,500 B.C.E., but what they left behind, bigger than life, tells a convincing tale of Goddess reverence. This Amulet image is of an entranceway to one of the temples at Hagar Qim. The overall interior structure of many of the temples takes the form of the Goddess with round, ample, generous curves. A bird's eye view shows two structures (among nearly thirty) in close proximity to each other, one larger than the other. Could they represent a mother and child figure? Considering the artifacts found in each temple, it could be that temples were used for different rituals; for instance, one may have been for birth ceremonies and another for death and regeneration.

Entrance stones, some measuring five by four yards, were carved with large double spiral designs also found at the gateways of many such megalithic temples elsewhere in Europe. Legends tell of a labyrinthine structure built deep below the surface. And an enormous underground "sanctuary" has been found.[16] The remains of one Goddess figure stands outside the temple; fully reconstructed, it would stand eighteen feet in height and weigh over two thousand tons.

When you receive the Temple Amulet you are about to take a big step. Some personal change has brought you to a critical place along your path. Perhaps an emotional crisis, an upset or an accident has transported you to another shore. You feel as if you had a near-death experience and just woke up. A memory of some hidden past event may have surfaced and surprised you. Shaken, you're a little wobbly on your feet. In terms of psychic healing the Goddess Temple actually foretells a new life unfolding.

You now need to focus your energy, taking care of any physical health issues before going on. Take time for a massage, yoga, quiet walks in nature or some other gentle form of healing body care. This is not the time for a rigorous workout. You must practice being *in* your body as if stepping into it for the first time. Take a bath. Eat slowly, meditating on each bite. Walk slowly, aware of each footstep as it touches the ground. The Temple Amulet often signals the call to shamanism. Once you are over the threshold, you may turn around like the wounded healer to help others through. Listen closely to find out what is calling you.

The Temple Amulet also represents the union of opposites, reminding the initiate to walk courageously between the stone pillars of the entranceway without bouncing from one extreme to the

Overview of limestone Goddess temple at Ggantija on the island of Gozo, near Malta. The egg-shaped outine is of a larger figure paired with a smaller one, similar to temple sites on Malta. Their juxtaposition suggests a mother and daughter or two sisters. This round, squat and bulbous shape also resembles Goddess sculptures found in many Maltese temples. The temples may represent the forces of birth and life, death and regeneration. The interior of the larger temple is decorated with spiral and snake carvings and includes a ritual hearth, altar tables and a red-painted alcove of stone slabs. Different rituals may have been performed in each temple according to the specific focus of the ceremony, performing seasonal celebrations and initiatory rites of birth, healing and death. (AB)

other. Live in the wholeness that contains the extremes.

Your breakthrough puts you more deeply in touch with Gaia, the Earth. You are awakening to compassionate responsibility for the environment and all creatures. Your own healing crisis has opened you to the heart of compassion. You see that you are part of a large-scale "eco-revolution." Most likely you've felt something coming for a long time, but you felt unsure about how you fit in. You may have had questions or doubts, or felt indifferent. Now you've connected your personal crisis with the environmental and global crisis. Focus your energy. You are a strong and passionate leader, mindful and skillful.

Once you cross the threshold, you are challenged to maintain a sense of balance. You can relax. You're home at last.

Goddesses: Dreaming Goddess of Malta, Gaia, Mami, Sita, Tacoma, Zemyna.

Images: Earth, water, nature, passageways, doorways, entrances.

Colors: Yellow ochre; the entire "family" of brown Earth tones.

Fragrance: Lavender (essential oil). Make a relaxing massage oil. Mix a few drops of lavender oil in a base of 1/4 cup canola oil, 1/8 cup almond oil, 1/8 cup jojoba oil. Experiment with the amount of lavender oil until it's just right for you.

Visualization/Meditation: Joining the Dance. Find a comfortable place to

Maltese Goddess of Regeneration from the Tarxien sanctuary. In Her original height, She would have stood over eighteen feet tall! Within the temples at Tarxien were found many animal, plant and spiral motifs. One animal figure is shown with thirteen "newborns" beneath her belly. All the art at Tarxien represents the overall theme of seasonal and cyclic renewal. (LM)

170 ❧ *Amulets of the Goddess*

sit. Rub some massage oil into your hands and face, inhaling the essence of lavender very deeply. Prop pillows all around you until you feel snug. Hold the Goddess Temple Amulet in your non-dominant hand. Breathe slowly.

Imagine standing at the entranceway to the temple. You feel the moist wind against your back, like a soft, large hand holding you gently, moving you forward. You take a slow step toward the portal. You hear a distant song and the beat of drums. You hear women's voices chanting rhythmically. The words are not clear. The sound pulls you forward another step. You reach out and press your hand against the rounded, warm stone. Each tiny crevice and worn hole is a witness to a mystery long past. You lift your head to the archway above. As you do, you catch the smell of flowers or the hint of perfume in the air.

You're halfway through the immense passageway. You feel the vibrations of a drumbeat against your bare feet. Each throbbing pulse echoes and bounces all around you. You lean against the wind and it gently encourages you toward the ancient sounds. You take another step into the song. Your heart pounds in time with the chanting beat. You take another step and you're in.

You now see the women dancing in a large open circle. Their dresses float in tune with the drum. Their hands are joined. They see you and smile. They nod their heads. It's as if they knew you were coming, and were waiting for you all along. Two women break their handhold, calling you to join them. You open your arms wide and join the dance. You stay for as long as you wish. Whenever you're ready, you return to your breath and the place where you are seated.

Use your journal to write your experience of the Temple Amulet meditation.

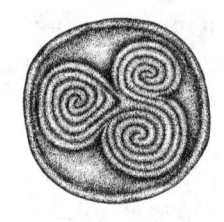

Triple Spiral—Barriers, Boundaries, and Possibilities

Spirals of every variation are the age-old symbol of the Goddess. Whether single spirals, moving inward and back out again, or as the more complex double and triple spirals, they represent birth and rebirth: being, knowing and becoming. The path leads an initiate into the dark womb of the Earth for divine communion (being) and returns along the same spiral path to rebirth (knowing) and re-entry (becoming).

This triple spiral motif is from Newgrange, County Meath, Ireland. It is carved on a megalithic stone, facing out eastward from the interior of the earthen mound. The entire structure is some quarter mile in circumference and fifty feet high. It was built to consecrate *place*. From there the movements of the Sun and Moon could be experienced. At Newgrange on the winter solstice, when the rising sun streams between the stones, it illuminates this triple spiral: Earth and Sun united at a moment in which celebrants participated and shared.

The triple spiral also refers to the threefold aspect of the Goddess as Maiden (Daughter), Mother and Crone. Metaphors for the Triple Goddess are known throughout every ancient matristic culture, translated in mythology, poetry and art. (See The Triple Goddess, Using Your Goddess Amulets, p. 42.) The Trinity was stolen, distorted and co-opted by many patriarchal religions, eliminating all traces of its origins and its association with female power.

When you receive the Triple Spiral, threefold action is suggested to change the situation you're in. If you're in a bind, unable to let go of the struggle long enough to see another approach, follow the spiral path...

▶ *Naming Barriers.* Make a list of the obstacles facing you. Which ones can you change? How would you change them? Which obstacles can't you change? Who are the people involved? What do you want to say to them? In your journal, answer the above questions. Clarifying the issues is the first step. Make yourself aware of the barriers and "blocks," diffusing the seemingly insurmountable power they contain. You may want to draw another Amulet at any time for further guidance.

▶ *Claiming Healthy Boundaries.* As you gain clarity, establish healthy boundaries as a step toward self-identity and self-love, essential elements in your relationships. This can help prevent the "doormat" syndrome where you don't know how to say "no," trying to be all things to all people. This is usually an approval-seeking mechanism. Set your own limits and call others who have stepped over the line. Be a healthy "parent" on your

Double and triple spiral motifs are prominent designs on the large stone (top) placed in front of the entrance to the complex archeological/astronomical site of Newgrange. Below, the uppermost roof box permits a narrow beam of sunlight to enter the chamber at sunrise on the Winter Solstice, illuminating the triple spiral at the very end of the long chamber, as well as other astronomical notations and symbolic stone carvings on its path. This cosmic event, when Earth, Sun and the human imagination are aligned, signals a dazzling moment of rebirth in the seasonal dance of time. (LM)

The Sacred Symbol Amulets: Triple Spiral ▶ *173*

own behalf. Say "no" when you have to; say "yes" when you want to.

🌀 *Creating Possibilities.* If you've been distracted, dancing to someone else's song, stop the music. Choreograph your own dance. Create new possibilities by doing it the way you want to do it, not the way you "should" do it. The spiral path is not two-dimensional. Either/or perspectives limit the scope of your potential. Trust your intuition and the wise Crone within for inspiration. Listen to the voice of your personal Muse.

> *Goddesses:* Brigit, The Fates, The Three Muses, Fortuna, Hera, Athena, Artemis, Aphrodite.
> *Colors:* White, red, black.
> *Fragrances:* Geranium (essential oil), gardenia (fresh flowers), bergamot (essential oil).
> *Gather Images That Evoke:* Cyclic, harmonious movement.
> *Creativity/Meditation:* Following the Spiral.

At the top of a large piece of paper, write the issue that you are struggling with. Draw a large triple spiral; title one of the spiral sections "Naming Barriers," the next "Healthy Boundaries," and the third "Creating Possibilities." Light a red or white candle. Inhale one of the suggested fragrances or one of your favorites. Relax, breathing deeply. Holding the Triple Spiral Amulet in your hand, gaze into it, without focusing on any one place in particular. Imagine dropping your consciousness deep into your belly. Visualize entering the spiral, the sacred and elemental map of the Goddess. As you travel through each section you can hear the voice of the Goddess whisper suggestions to you about how to solve your problem. When you come around to the third section of the spiral, a ray of sunlight illuminates your path. On the ground before you, a word is scratched in the sand; its meaning comforts you.

Write your experiences from your journey in the appropriate sections of your paper.

Whirlwinds — Trusting the Invisible

This image of a whirling design around a butterfly in the shape of a double axe is from a Minoan pottery dish, 5,000 B.C.E. In Goddess cultures throughout Old Europe and the Mediterranean, symbols of movement and transformation were often depicted by swirls, spirals and patterns resembling currents. Whatever the motif, the metaphor is motion.

According to Marija Gimbutas (who extensively researched the symbols of early Neolithic Mother Goddess cultures of Old Europe), whirling images, wavy patterns and symbols of motion are visual metaphors for transformation and transition, thwarting stagnation. In agricultural communities dependent on seasonal growth, life takes place amid the recognition of cyclical change.

The butterfly image in the center of the whirlwinds may represent the human soul, rebirth and the ability to change from an incomplete chrysalis into a marvelous and beautiful creature. Butterfly images in the form of double axes abound as symbols of transformation in Cretan art and arti-

Shaman/priestess from Crete with enlarged hands, each finger a receptor and transmitter of divine energy. She is able to commune with the spirit world while her body seems stable, rooted in the earth. Her guardian spirit bird sits atop her head. (AB)

The Sacred Symbol Amulets: Whirlwinds

facts. The hexagon in the center creates a protective border around the human spirit.

The five "fingers" of the whirlwinds may relate to the Dactyls, shamans of early Crete who performed ceremonies of initiation and renewal.[17] They personified the hands of the Great Goddess. Many images of the Goddess from this period show Her with arms upraised and oversized hands seemingly emanating divine energy.[18] Through Her gift of loving touch, the Goddess made and moved all life.

When you get the Whirlwinds Amulet, you may not be able to see tangible proof or reap an immediate reward, but your efforts have definitely influenced your environment. You may be used to wanting and expecting immediate results and gratification, but you can't expect to pick fruit the day you plant the tree. Every idea and inspiration has a gestation period beginning in the realm of the invisible. If the winds of change brought everything you wanted at once, you would be overwhelmed, caught in a hurricane of events; you would inevitably sabotage yourself. The gentle hands of the Goddess will bring you what you need when you need it. Keep your eye on "indirect" and subtle responses, like the wind that moves the branches of a tree. Trust the invisible. Disconnect yourself from the storms that may be distracting you. Find your center.

Having done your groundwork, you have nothing to fear. "Luck" happens *only* when preparation meets opportunity. While waiting in the still moments before your flowers blossom, continue to work the fertile ground of your plan. You have already set the forces in motion for accom-

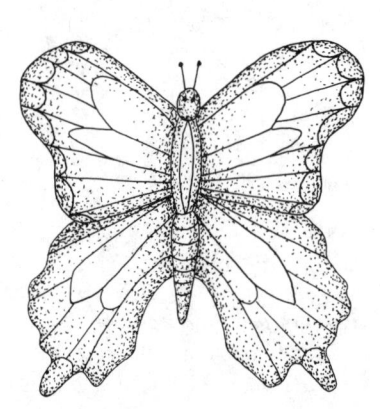

The butterfly is a symbol of rebirth and renewal, power held in the hands of the Goddess and Her priestesses who performed healing magic in the realm of the invisible. (AB)

plishing it—whether by thinking the thoughts, speaking the words, or using the tools to implement action. Make sure that your plan is clear to you so the forces of change can follow your course accordingly. Your Goddess Guides remind you to keep your vision alive, nurturing it every step of the way, especially during the quiet times. Just as a butterfly larva continues to nurture itself in the darkness while building for an awesome and beautiful flight, you too must keep your outcome in mind, no matter what is going on around you.

Goddesses: Aradia, Cardea, Shekinah, Ninlil, Nut, Tatsuta-Hime, Savitri, Urania, Kuan Yin, Tara.
Gather Images That Evoke: Stillness, calm, trust in the forces of divine immanence.
Colors: Violet, clear, white.
Fragrances: Carnation (fresh flowers), vanilla (ground beans).
Visualization/Meditation: In The Whirlwinds.

Crush a few vanilla beans and rub them into the Whirlwinds Amulet. Sit quietly, inhaling the fragrance deeply with the Amulet in your hand. Take long deep breaths, holding for three seconds between inhaling and exhaling. Focus your attention on the Whirlwinds image. Imagine that you are standing in the very center of the hexagon. Observe the stillness. Your arms outstretched, you feel protected and safe. Whatever plans you have recently put in motion are represented by the swirling "fingers of fate" around you. Their invisible action invokes subtle and powerful transformative energy. Like ripples from a pebble tossed in a pond, the waves generate out from your center. You feel profound trust knowing the forces are in your favor.

> We come from the Whirlwinds
> Living in the Whirlwinds
> Go back to the Whirlwinds
> Turn your world around

Notes

Using Your Goddess Amulets
1. Starhawk, *Truth or Dare*. San Francisco: HarperCollins, 1989, p. 98.
2. Mary Daly, *Pure Lust: Elemental Feminist Philosophy*. Boston: Beacon Press, 1984, p. 11.
3. Gloria Orenstein, *Reflowering of the Goddess*. New York: Macmillan, 1990, p. 23.
4. Vicki Noble, *Motherpeace: A Way to the Goddess Through Myth, Art and Tarot*. New York: Harper & Row, 1983, pp. 29-34.
5. Susan Griffin, *Pornography and Silence: Culture's Revenge Against Nature*. New York: Harper & Row, 1981, p. 1.
6. Barbara G. Walker, *The Woman's Encyclopedia of Myths and Secrets*. San Francisco: Harper & Row, 1983, p. 1018.
7. Susun S. Weed, *Healing Wise*. Woodstock, NY: Ash Tree Publishing, 1989, pp. 78-9.
8. Ibid., pp. 79-80.

The Goddess Amulets
1. Demetra George, *Mysteries of the Dark Moon*. San Francisco: HarperCollins, 1992, p. 159.
2. Ibid., p. 155.
3. Ibid., p. 162.
4. Vicki Noble, *Shakti Woman*. San Francisco: HarperCollins, 1991, p. 28.
5. Yoko Ono, "Rainbow Revelation," from her album *Star Peace*. Copyright © 1985 by Ono Music.
6. Diane Wolkstein and Samuel Noah Kramer, *Inanna: Queen of Heaven and Earth*. New York: Harper & Row, 1983, p. 127.
7. Ibid., p. xvi.

8. Sylvia Perera, *Descent to the Goddess*. Toronto: Inner City Books, 1981, p. 14.
9. Wolkstein and Kramer, op. cit., p. 52.
10. Alexander Marshack, *Roots of Civilization*. Mt. Kisco, NY: Moyer Bell Ltd., 1991, p. 335.
11. Merlin Stone. *When God Was a Woman*. San Diego: Harcourt Brace Jovanovich, 1976, p. 201.
12. Henri Frankfort, *Kingship and the Gods*. Chicago: University of Chicago Press, 1968, p. 67. Quoted in Anne Baring and Jules Cashford, *The Myth of the Goddess*. New York: Viking, 1991, p. 125.
13. Patricia Monaghan, *The Book of Goddesses & Heroines*. St Paul, MN: Llewellyn, 1990, p. 222.
14. Erich Neumann, *The Great Mother: An Analysis of the Archetype*. Ralph Manheim, trans. Princeton, NJ: Princeton University Press, 1955, p. 133.
15. Judith Duerk, *Circle of Stones*. San Diego: LuraMedia, 1989, p. 14.
16. Noble, *Shakti Woman*, p. 13.
17. R. Gordon Wasson, George Cowan, Florence Cowan and Willard Rhodes, *Maria Sabina and Her Mazatec Mushroom Velada*. San Diego: Harcourt Brace Jovanovich, 1974, pp. 17-206. Quoted in Joan Halifax, *Shamanic Voices*. New York: Penguin Books USA, 1991, p. 4.
18. Ibid.
19. Ibid, p. 5.
20. Monica Sjöö and Barbara Mor, *The Great Cosmic Mother*. San Francisco: HarperCollins, 1987, p. 54.
21. Halifax, op. cit., pp. 196-213.
22. Sjöö and Mor, op. cit., pp. 320-1.
23. Brian Branston, *Lost Gods of England*. London: Thames and Hudson, 1984, p. 154.
24. Walker, *Woman's Encyclopedia*, p. 931-2.
25. Barbara G. Walker, *The Woman's Dictionary of Sacred Symbols and Objects*. San Francisco: HarperCollins, 1988, p. 235.
26. Ibid., p. 236.
27. Rachel G. Levy, *Religious Conceptions of the Stone Age and Their Influence Upon European Thought*. New York: Harper & Row, 1963, p. 65.

The Sacred Animal Amulets

1. Buffie Johnson, *Lady of the Beasts*. San Francisco: HarperCollins, 1990, p. 106.
2. Joseph L. Henderson and Maud Oakes, *The Wisdom of the Serpent: The Myths of Death, Rebirth, and Resurrection*. Princeton, NJ: Princeton University Press, 1990, p. 257.
3. Lawrence Durdin-Robertson, *God The Mother: The Creatress and Giver of Life*. Clonegal Castle, Enniscorthy, Eire: Cesara Publications, MMMMCCCXXXII, p. 31.
4. Walker, *Woman's Encyclopedia*, p. 181.
5. Ibid.
6. Marija Gimbutas, *The Language of the Goddess*. San Francisco: HarperCollins, 1989, p. 265.
7. Ibid., p. 267.
8. Riane Eisler, *The Chalice & The Blade: Our History, Our Future*. San Francisco: HarperCollins, 1988, p.105.
9. Gimbutas, op. cit., pp. 251-2.
10. E.A. Wallis Budge, *Egyptian Magic*. New York: Dover, 1971, p. 61. Quoted in Barbara G. Walker, *The Woman's Dictionary of Sacred Symbols and Objects*. San Francisco: HarperCollins, 1988, p. 375.
11. Gimbutas, op. cit., p. 256.
12. Walker, *Woman's Encyclopedia*, p. 754.
13. Johnson, op. cit., p. 36.
14. Walker, *Woman's Encyclopedia*, p. 904.
15. Ibid.
16. Johnson, op. cit., pp. 170-171.
17. Ibid.
18. Ibid., p. 172.
19. Sjöö and Mor, op. cit., p. 58.
20. Ibid., citing Marcia Patrick, *Earthly Origins*, 1983 unpublished manuscript, p. 249.
21. Johnson, op. cit., p. 178.
22. Ibid.
23. Hallie Iglehart Austen, *The Heart of the Goddess*. Berkeley, CA: Wingbow Press, 1990, pp. 50-51.
25. Gimbutas, op. cit., p. 146.
26. Walker, *Woman's Encylopedia*, p. 956.
27. Ibid.
28. Johnson, op. cit., p. 211.

The Sacred Symbol Amulets

1. Gimbutas, op. cit., p. 293.
2. Johnson, op. cit., p. 42.
3. Walker, *Women's Encyclopedia*, p. 349.
4. Ibid., p. 368, citing P. Rawson, *Erotic Art of the East*. New York: G.P. Putnam's Sons, 1968, p. 67.
5. Gimbutas, op. cit., p. 53.
6. Emily Culpepper, "Female History/Myth Making," *The Second Wave*, Volume 4, No. 1 1075, pp. 14-17.
7. Gimbutas, op. cit., p. 53.
8. Walker, *Women's Encyclopedia*, p. 295.
9. Gimbutas, op. cit., p. 306.
10. Sjöö and Mor, op. cit., p. 247.
11. Walker, *Women's Encyclopedia*, p. 25.
12. Norma Lorre Goodrich, *Priestesses*. New York: HarperCollins, 1989.
13. Starhawk, *The Spiral Dance*. San Francisco: HarperCollins, 1989, p. 91.
14. Gimbutas, op. cit., p. 101.
15. Ibid., p. 102, citing Marie-Louise von Franz in *Problems of the Feminine in Fairytales*. Dallas: Spring Publications, 1972, p. 38.
16. Sjöö and Mor, op. cit., p. 112.
17. Johnson, op. cit., p. 194.
18. Ibid.

Bibliography and Other Sources

Achterberg, Jeanne. *Imagery in Healing: Shamanism and Modern Medicine.* Boston: Shambhala, 1985.

Adler, Margot. *Drawing Down The Moon: Witches, Druids, Goddess-Worshippers, and Other Pagans in America Today.* Boston: Beacon Press, 1986.

Allen, Paula Gunn. *The Sacred Hoop: Recovering the Feminine in American Indian Traditions.* Boston: Beacon Press, 1986.

—. *Spider Woman's Granddaughters.* Boston: Beacon Press, 1989.

Arguelles, Jose and Miriam Arguelles. *Mandala.* Boston: Shambhala, 1972.

Austen, Hallie Iglehart. *The Heart Of The Goddess: Art, Myth and Meditations of the World's Sacred Feminine.* Berkeley, CA: Wingbow Press, 1990.

Azara, Nancy. Psychic Healing Workshops given in New York, 1984-1986.

Baring, Anne and Jules Cashford. *The Myth of the Goddess: Evolution of an Image.* New York: Viking Arkana, 1991.

Beattie, Melody. *Codependent No More: How to Stop Controlling Others and Start Caring for Yourself.* New York: Harper/Hazelden, 1987.

—. *Beyond Codependence and Getting Better All the Time.* San Francisco: Harper & Row, 1989.

—. *The Language of Letting Go.* Meditation Tape. Hazelden, 1990.

Blair, Nancy. *Art and the Healing Process: Workshops for Women.* Unpublished Papers, 1988-1990.

—. *The Great Goddess Collection Gift Catalog.* North Brunswick, New Jersey: Star River Productions, Inc., 1991.

—. *Psychic Circle, Meditations And Visualizations.* Unpublished Papers, 1985-1988.

—. "Woman's Spirituality." *Fellowship In Prayer*, Vol. 39, No. 6, December 1988.

Blum, Ralph. *The Book of Runes: A Handbook for the Use of an Ancient Oracle: The Viking Runes*. New York: St. Martin's Press, 1987.

Branston, Brian. *The Lost Gods Of England*. London: Thames and Hudson, 1984.

Brennan, Martin. *The Stars and the Stones: Ancient Art and Astronomy in Ireland*. London: Thames and Hudson, 1983.

Buckland, Raymond. *Practical Color Magick*. St Paul, MN: Llewellyn, 1985.

Budapest, Zsuzsanna E. *Grandmother Moon: Lunar Magic in Our Lives*. San Francisco: HarperCollins Publishers, 1991.

—. *The Holy Book of Women's Mysteries*. Berkeley, CA: Wingbow Press, 1989.

Budge, E.A. Wallis. *Amulets And Superstitions*. New York: Dover Publications, Inc., 1978.

—. *Egyptian Magic*. New York: Dover Publications, 1971.

Campbell, Joseph. *The Way of the Animal Powers*, Vol. 1. London: Alfred van der Marck, 1983.

Carlson, Ph.D., Richard and Benjamin Shield. *Healers on Healing*. Los Angeles: Jeremy P. Tarcher, Inc., 1989.

Cheatham, Annie, and Mary Clare Powell. *This Way Daybreak Comes*. Philadelphia: New Society Publishers, 1986.

Chernin, Kim. *The Hungry Self: Women, Eating & Identity*. New York: Harper & Row, 1985.

—. *The Obsession: Reflections on the Tyranny of Slenderness*. New York: Harper & Row, 1981.

—. *Reinventing Eve: Modern Woman in Search of Herself*. New York: Times Books, 1987.

Crawford, O.G.S. *The Eye Goddess*. New York: Macmillan, 1957.

Culpepper, Emily. "Female History/Myth Making," *The Second Wave*, Volume 4, No. 1 1075.

Cunningham, Scott. *Magical Aromatheraphy: The Power Of Scent*. St. Paul, MN: Llewellyn, 1992.

Daly, Mary. *Beyond God the Father: Toward a Philosophy of Women's Liberation*. Boston: Beacon Press, 1973.

—. *Gyn/ecology: The Metaethics of Radical Feminism*. Boston: Beacon Press, 1978.

—. *Pure Lust: Elemental Feminist Philosophy*. Boston: Beacon Press, 1984.

—. *Webster's First New Intergalactic Wickedary Of The English Language*. Boston: Beacon Press, 1987.

Davis, Patricia. *Aromatherapy: An A-Z*. Saffron Walden, England: C.W. Daniel Co. Ltd., 1988.

Demetrakopoulos, Stephanie. *Listening To Our Bodies: The Rebirth Of Feminine Wisdom*. Boston: Beacon Press, 1983.

Downing, Christine. *The Goddess: Mythological Images of the Feminine*. New York: Crossroad, 1990.

Duerk, Judith. *Circle of Stones: Woman's Journey To Herself*. San Diego, CA: LuraMedia, 1989.

Durdin-Robertson, Lawrence. *God The Mother: The Creatress and Giver of Life*. Clonegal Castle, Enniscorthy, Eire: Cesara Publications, MMMMCCCXXXII.

Ehrenreich, Barbara and Deirdre English. *Witches, Midwives and Nurses. A History of Women Healers*. New York: The Feminist Press, 1973.

Eisler, Riane. *The Chalice & The Blade: Our History, Our Future*. San Francisco: HarperCollins Publishers, 1988.

Evans-Pritchard, E.E. *Witchcraft, Oracles And Magic Among The Azande*. Oxford: Clarendon Press, 1965.

Faludi, Susan. *Backlash: The Undeclared War Against American Woman*. New York: Crown Publishers, Inc., 1991.

Fox, Matthew, ed. *Hildegard of Bingen's Book Of Divine Works*. Santa Fe, NM: Bear & Company, 1987.

Frazer, Sir James George. *The Golden Bough: A Study in Magic and Religion*. New York: Macmillan, 1951.

Gadon, Elinor W. *The Once & Future Goddess*. New York: Harper & Row, 1989.

Gendlin, Eugene T. *Focusing*. New York: Everest House, 1978.

George, Demetra. *Mysteries of the Dark Moon: The Healing Power of The Dark Goddess*. San Francisco: HarperCollins, 1992.

Gersi, Douchan. *Faces in the Smoke: An Eyewitness Experience of Voodoo, Shamanism, Psychic Healing, and Other Amazing Human Powers*. Los Angeles: Jeremy P. Tarcher, 1991.

Getty, Adele. *Goddess: Mother of Living Nature*. New York: Thames and Hudson, 1990.

Gibson, Walter B. and Litzka R. Gibson. *The Complete Illustrated Book of Divination and Prophecy*. Garden City, NY: Doubleday, 1973.

Gimbutas, Marija. *The Language Of The Goddess*. San Francisco: Harper & Row, 1989.

—. *The Civilization of the Goddess*. San Francisco: HarperCollins, 1991.

Goodrich, Norma Lorre. *Priestesses*. New York: Franklin Watts, 1989.

Graves, Robert. *The White Goddess*. New York: Farrar, Straus and Giroux, 1987.

Great Goddess Collective. *The Great Goddess*. New York: Heresies, a Feminist Publication on Art & Politics, 1982.

Green, Miranda. *Symbol & Image In Celtic Religious Art*. New York: Routledge, Chapman and Hall, 1989.

Griffin, Susan. *Pornography And Silence: Culture's Revenge Against Nature*. New York: Harper & Row, 1981.

Halifax, Joan, ed. *Shamanic Voices: A Survey of Visionary Narratives*. New York: E.P. Dutton, 1979.

—. *Shaman: The Wounded Healer*. New York: Crossroad, 1982.

Hammond, Harmony. *Wrappings: Essays on Feminism, Art, and the Martial Arts*. New York: Mussmann Bruce Publishers, 1984.

Hanon, Geraldine Hatch. *Sacred Space: A Feminist Vision Of Astrology*. New York: Firebrand Books, 1990.

Henderson, Joseph L. and Maude Oakes. *The Wisdom of the Serpent: The Myths of Death, Rebirth and Resurrection*. Princeton, NJ: Princeton University Press, 1990.

Hoffmann, David. *The Holistic Herbal*. Element Books, 1983.

Hutchinson, Marcia Germaine. *Transforming Body Image: Learning To Love The Body You Have*. Trumansburg, NY: Crossing Press, 1985.

Iglehart, Hallie Austen. *Womanspirit: A Guide To Woman's Wisdom*. San Francisco: Harper & Row, 1983.

Janson, H. W. with Dora Jane Janson. *The History of Art: A Survey of the Major Visual Arts from the Dawn of History to the Present Day*. Englewood Cliffs, NJ: Prentice Hall, 1962.

Johnson, Buffie. *Lady of the Beasts: Ancient Images of the Goddess and Her Sacred Animals*. San Francisco: HarperCollins, 1988.

Johnson, Sonia. *The Ship That Sailed Into The Living Room: Sex and Intimacy Reconsidered*. Escancia, NM: Wildfire Books, 1991.

Kaster, Joseph. *Putnam's Concise Mythological Dictionary*. New York: G.P. Putnam, 1980.

Kelly, Michele. Weekly conversations about Addiction, Goddess Spirituality, and Healing. New Jersey, 1990-92.

Koltuv, Ph.D., Barbara Black. *The Book of Lilith*. York Beach, ME: Nicolas-Hayes, Inc., 1986.

Kunz, Dora, ed. *Spiritual Aspects Of The Healing Arts*. Wheaton, IL: Theosophical Publishing House, 1985.

Larsen, Earnie and Carol Hegarty Larsen. *Days of Healing, Days of Joy: Daily Meditations for Adult Children*. San Francisco: Hazelden/HarperCollins, 1987.

Lauter, Estelle. *Women as Mythmakers: Poetry and Visual Art by Twentieth-Century Women*. Bloomington, IN: Indiana University Press, 1984.

Leonard, Linda Schierse. *Witness To The Fire: Creativity And the Veil of Addiction*. Boston: Shambhala, 1989.

Lerner, Ph.D., Harriet Goldnor. *The Dance of Anger*. New York: Harper & Row, 1985.

Leroi-Gourhan, Andre. *Treasures Of Prehistoric Art*. New York: Harry N. Abrams, 1967.

Levy, Rachel G. *Religious Conceptions of the Stone Age and Their Influence Upon European Thought*. New York: Harper & Row, 1963.

Lippard, Lucy R. *From The Center: Feminist Essays on Women's Art*. New York: E.P. Dutton, 1976.

—. *Get The Message? A Decade of Art For Social Change*. New York: E.P. Dutton, Inc., 1984.

—. *Overlay: Contemporary Art and the Art of Prehistory*. New York: Pantheon Books, 1983.

Lorde, Audre. *Sister Outsider*. Trumansburg, NY: Crossing Press, 1984.

The Lunar Calendar, Dedicated to the Goddess in Her Many Guises. Published annually by Luna Press, Boston.

Mariechild, Diane. *Mother Wit: A Feminist Guide to Psychic Development*. Trumansburg, NY: Crossing Press, 1981.

Marshack, Alexander. *The Roots of Civilization*. Mount Kisco, NY: Moyer Bell Limited, 1991.

Matthews, Caitlin. *Sophia, Goddess of Wisdom: The Divine Feminine from Black Goddess to World-Soul*. London: HarperCollins, 1991.

Mellaart, James. *Çatal Huyuk: A Neolithic Town in Anatolia*. New York: McGraw-Hill, 1967.

Michell, John. *Megalithomania: Artists, Antiquarians and Archaeologists at the Old Stone Monuments*. Ithaca, NY: Cornell University Press, 1982.

Miller, Jean Baker. *Toward a New Psychology of Women*. Boston: Beacon Press, 1976.

Miller, Richard Alan and Iona Miller. *The Magical and Ritual Use of Perfumes*. Rochester, VT: Destiny Books, 1990.

Monaghan, Patricia. *The Book Of Goddess & Heroines*. St Paul, MN: Llewellyn, 1990.

Mookerjee, Ajit. *Kali: The Feminine Force*. Rochester, VT: Destiny Books, 1988.

Mountainwater, Shekhinah. *Ariadne's Thread: A Workbook of Goddess Magic*. Freedom, CA: Crossing Press, 1991.

Murdock, Maureen. *The Heroine's Journey*. Boston: Shambhala, 1990.

Neumann, Erich. *The Great Mother: An Analysis of the Archetype*. Ralph Manheim, trans. Princeton, NJ: Princeton University Press, 1955.

Nicholson, Shirley, ed. *The Goddess Re-Awakening: The Feminine Principle Today*. London: Theosophical Publishing House, 1989.

Noble, Vicki. *Motherpeace: A Way to the Goddess through Myth, Art and Tarot*. San Francisco: HarperCollins, 1983.

—. *Shakti Woman: Feeling Our Fire, Healing Our World — The New Female Shamanism*. San Francisco: HarperCollins, 1991.

Orenstein, Gloria Feman. *The Reflowering of the Goddess*. New York: Pergamon Press, 1990.

—. *Creation And Healing: An Empowering Relationship For Women Artists*. Women's Studies Int. Forum. Vol. 8, No. 5, 1985. Printed in Great Britain.

Pagels, Elaine. *The Gnostic Gospels*. New York: Random House, Inc., 1989.

Perera, Sylvia Brinton. *Descent to the Goddess: A Way of Initiation for Women*. Toronto: Inner City Books, 1981.

Plaskow, Judith, and Carol P. Christ, eds. *Weaving the Visions: New Patterns in Feminist Spirituality*. San Francisco: HarperCollins, 1989.

Purce, Jill. *The Mystic Spiral: Journey of the Soul*. New York: Thames and Hudson, 1980.

Rawson, P. *Erotic Art of the East*. New York: G.P. Putnam, 1968.

Redmond, Layne. Frame Drumming Workshop at The Center For Symbolic Studies, New York, June 1991.

The Return of the Goddess Engagement Calendar. Published annually by Hands of the Goddess Press, Amherst MA.

Rufus, Anneli S. and Kristan Lawson. *Goddess Sites: Europe*. San Francisco: HarperCollins, 1990.

Rush, Anne Kent. *Getting Clear: Body Work for Women.* New York: Random House, 1973.

—. *Moon, Moon.* New York: Random House, 1976.

Sams, Jamie and David Carson. *Medicine Cards: The Discovery of Power Through the Ways of Animals.* Santa Fe, NM: Bear & Company, 1988.

Schaef, Anne Wilson. *Meditations For Women Who Do Too Much.* San Francisco: HarperCollins, 1990.

Schenkel, Susan, Ph.D. *Giving Away Success: Why Women Get Stuck and What To Do About It.* New York: HarperCollins, 1991.

Shuttle, Penelope and Peter Redgrove. *The Wise Wound: Myths, Realities, and Meanings of Menstruation.* New York: Bantam Books, 1990.

Sjöö, Monica and Barbara Mor. *The Great Cosmic Mother: Rediscovering The Religion Of The Earth.* San Francisco: HarperCollins, 1991.

Small, Jacquelyn. *Awakening In Time: The Journey from Codependence to Co-Creation.* New York: Bantam Books, 1991.

Spangler, David and William Irwin Thompson. *Reimagination of the World: A Critique of the New Age, Science, and Popular Culture.* Santa Fe, NM: Bear & Company, 1991.

Spretnak, Charlene. *Lost Goddesses of Early Greece: A Collection of Pre-Hellenic Mythology.* Boston: Beacon Press, 1978.

—, ed. *The Politics of Women's Spirituality.* Garden City, NY: Doubleday, 1982.

Starhawk. *Dreaming The Dark: Magic, Sex & Politics.* Boston: Beacon Press, 1982.

—. *The Spiral Dance: A Rebirth of the Ancient Religion of the Great Goddess.* New York: Harper & Row, 1979.

—. *Truth or Dare: Encounters with Power, Authority, and Mystery.* New York: Harper & Row, 1987.

Stein, Diane. *All Women Are Healers: A Comprehensive Guide to Natural Healing.* Freedom, CA: Crossing Press, 1990.

Stone, Merlin. *Ancient Mirrors Of Womanhood: A Treasury of Goddess and Heroine Lore From Around the World.* Boston: Beacon Press, 1990.

—. *When God Was a Woman.* San Diego: Harcourt Brace Jovanovich, 1976.

Tavris, Carol. *Anger, the Misunderstood Emotion.* New York: Simon & Schuster, 1982.

Taylor, Dena & Amber Coverdale Sumrall, eds. *Women of the 14th Moon: Writings on Menopause.* Freedom, CA: Crossing Press, 1991.

Teish, Luisah. *Jambalaya: the Natural Woman's Book of Personal Charms & Practical Rituals*. San Francisco: Harper & Row, 1985.

Thomas, William & Kate Pavitt. *The Book Of Talismans, Amulets and Zodiacal Gems*. N. Hollywood, CA: Wilshire Book Co., 1970.

Thorsten, Geraldine. *The Goddess In Your Stars: The Original Feminine Meanings Of The Sun Signs*. New York: Simon & Schuster, 1989.

Von Franz, Marie-Louise. *On Divination and Synchronicity: The Psychology of Meaningful Chance*. Toronto: Inner City Books, 1980.

Von Rosen, Lissie. *Lapis Lazuli in Geological Contexts and in Ancient Written Sources*. Sweden: Paul Astroms Forlag, 1988.

Walker, Barbara G. *The Crone: Woman of Age, Wisdom, and Power*. San Francisco: Harper & Row, 1985.

—. *The Woman's Dictionary of Symbols and Sacred Objects*. San Francisco: Harper & Row, 1988.

—. *The Woman's Encyclopedia of Myths and Secrets*. San Francisco: Harper & Row, 1983.

—. *Women's Rituals: A Sourcebook*. New York: Harper & Row, 1990.

Wasson, R. Gordon, George Cowan, Florence Cowan and Willard Rhodes. *Maria Sabina and Her Mazatec Mushroom Velada*. San Diego: Harcourt Brace Jovanovich, 1974.

We'Moon, Gaia Rhythms: An Astrological Moon Calendar, Appointment Book, and Daily Guide to Natural Rhythm for Wemoon. Published annually by Mother Tongue Ink, Estacada, OR.

Weed, Susun S. *Healing Wise*. Woodstock, NY: Ash Tree Publishing, 1989.

—. *Wise Woman Ways for the Menopausal Years*. Woodstock, NY: Ash Tree Publishing, 1992.

Wolkstein, Diane and Samuel Noah Kramer. *Inanna: Queen of Heaven and Earth*. New York: Harper & Row, 1983.

About the Author

Nancy Blair is a visionary artist and teacher. She graduated from Alfred University and received her M.F.A. from Rutgers University, Mason Gross School of the Arts. She has taught ceramics at Rutgers and will be teaching at the Wise Woman Center in Woodstock, New York. Her artwork has been exhibited in solo and group shows in New York and other cities, and her poems, artwork and reviews have been published in arts and women's publications. She leads workshops and rituals on the Goddess, creativity and healing.

Nancy teaches that art is sacred—direct communication with the Divine—and that creativity and artmaking are powerful shamanic healing processes. "The Goddess has been the most powerful source of healing in my life."

Her company, Star River Productions, The Great Goddess Collection, has sold Goddess art since 1986. For information on workshops and to receive a copy of The Great Goddess Collection Gift Catalog, write Star River Productions, PO Box 7754, North Brunswick, NJ 08902.